# DRAWING THE DRAPED FIGURE
## (THE SEVEN LAWS OF FOLDS)

GEORGE B. BRIDGMAN

DOVER PUBLICATIONS
Garden City, New York

## PUBLISHER'S NOTE

George Bridgman is considered by some to have been the greatest teacher of figure drawing of his day. An inspiration to generations of students in his classes at the Art Students League in New York, he taught thousands more through his many books, of which *Drawing the Draped Figure* is the sixth to be published by Dover. These books are proving as popular now as when they were first published. Read together, they make a complete course in the representation of the human form in classical style.

*Bibliographical Note*

This Dover edition, first published in 2001, is an unabridged republication of the original edition published by Bridgman Publishers, Inc., Pelham, New York, under the title *The Seven Laws of Folds* in 1942.

*Library of Congress Cataloging-in-Publication Data*

Bridgman, George Brant, 1864–1943.
    Drawing the draped figure : The seven laws of folds / George B. Bridgman.
        p. cm.
    Originally published: The seven laws of folds. 1st ed. Pelham, N.Y. : Bridgman Publishers, 1942.
    ISBN-13: 978-0-486-41802-5 (pbk.)
    ISBN-10: 0-486-41802-2 (pbk.)
    1. Drapery in art. 2. Figure drawing—Technique. I. Title: Seven laws of folds. II. Bridgman, George Brant, 1864–1943. Seven laws of folds. III. Title.

NC775 .B7 2001
743.5—dc21
                                                                    2001028649

Printed in Canada
41802217    2025
www.doverpublications.com

# FOREWORD

CLOTHING is none other than drapery arranged around a body that is beneath it. To express the multitudinous forms it takes, one should learn to express in a direct way the different characters of folds, for each one plays its individual part as distinctly apart as actors play their different characters upon the stage.

Folds are totally different. There are those which pass around and radiate from the points of support, clasping the figure thereby reducing the receding surface to a minimum or they may zigzag in an irregular manner from side to side. There are folds which are straight, festooned and V shaped; folds which fall, cross or pass around the figure. There are materials which have concave and convex forms as well as cord-like edges. All folds have laws unto themselves. Some folds run into their opponents and die away while there are others which terminate abruptly. Each individual fold has its own manner, its temperament and almost its religion. Each pursues its function so that each must be studied apart as a fixed law, a thing entirely apart, without connection, yet held throughout by the unforeseen laws of rhythm.

As you would study the surface or an arm and forearm, or a thigh and a leg and their connection at the elbow or at the knee joints, these folds must come together, linked as they pass around or into one another. To do so, a name indicating a function must be given to each.

1. PIPE
2. ZIGZAG
3. SPIRAL
4. HALF-LOCK
5. DIAPER PATTERN
6. DROP
7. INERT

In the following pages it is hoped that their meaning will be made clear.

DEDICATED TO

ELEANOR BLAIR

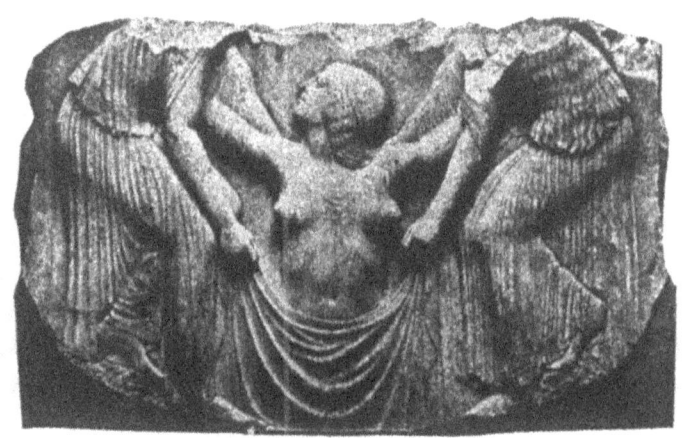

# CONTENTS

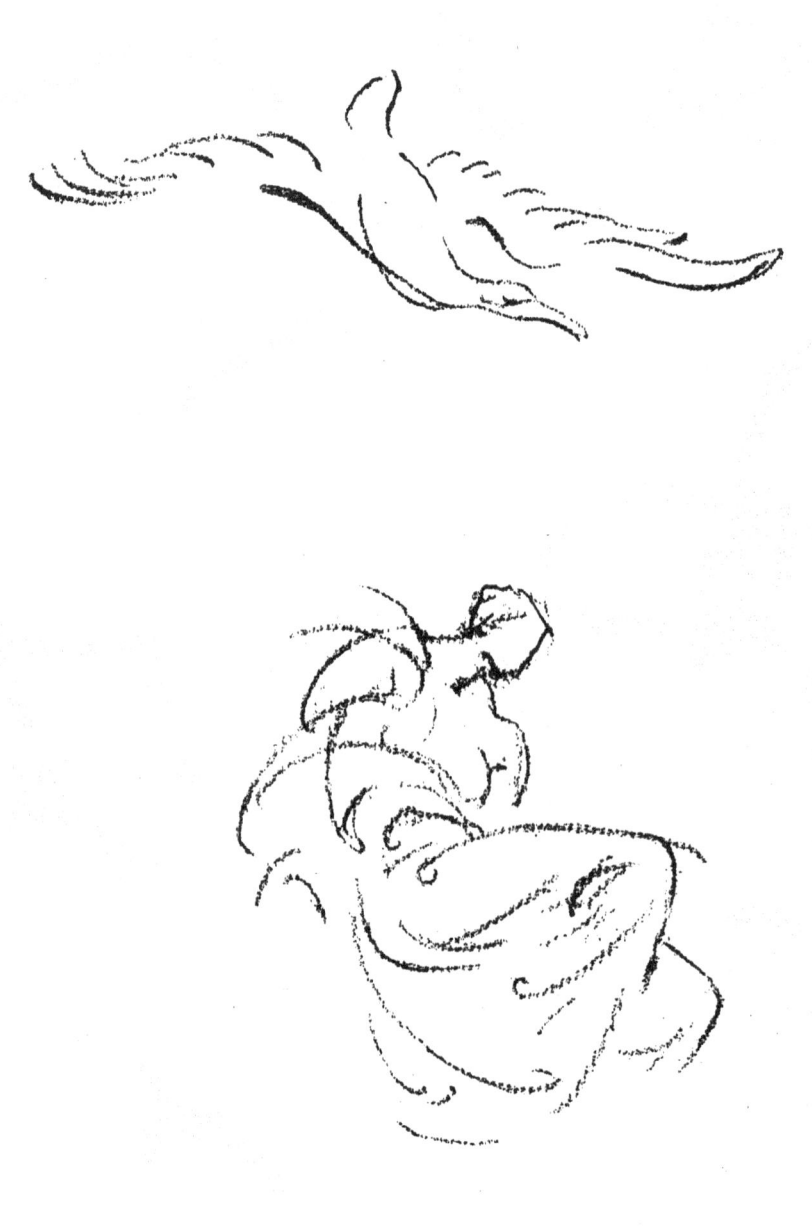

# RHYTHM

THE arrangement of line and volume of folds is not complete or harmonious without a hidden and subtle flow of symmetry. Nature has supplied both line and form that are symmetrical and harmonious. These laws of rhythm exist and are recognized as undefined laws.

There is rhythm in the movement of the sea and tides, in stars and planets, in trees and grasses, clouds and thistledown. It is a part of all animal and plant life. It is the movement of uttered words expressed in their accented and unaccented syllables and in the grouping and pauses of speech. Both poetry and music are the embodiment in appropriate rhythmical sound; of beautiful thought; imagination or emotion. Without rhythm there could be no poetry or music. In drawing and painting there is rhythm in outline, color, light and shade. So to express rhythm in drawing a figure we have in the balance of masses, a subordination of the passive or inactive side, to the more forceful and angular side in action, keeping constantly in mind the hidden, subtle flow of symmetry throughout.

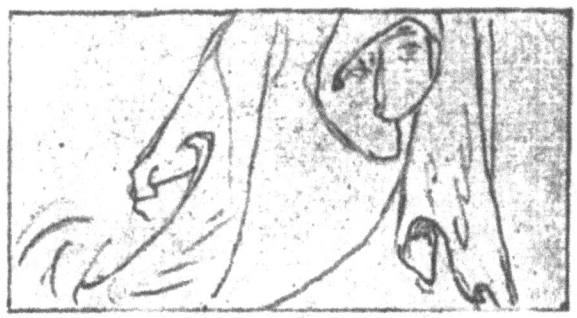

Many teachers and art students should be glad to have some definite knowledge of folds and should be pleased to have some idea that explains the principles which underlie the various forms that take place on the draped figure. To make this clear and as simple as possible, diagrams are shown by way of illustrations that are founded upon important truths. These primary principles are built upon the theory that each fold has a different function and character.

There has been a great lack of concise and simple understanding on the subject. Much that has heretofore been written, has for the most part, been vague and of little educational value.

The diagrams on pages eight and nine come under the head of geometric or working drawings and represent seven distinct characters of folds, each playing its individual role in the story of the draped human body.

One can make a code of laws to be governed by, but every one of these can be changed or eliminated, still one should know these laws so that they may be used as such or deliberately broken.

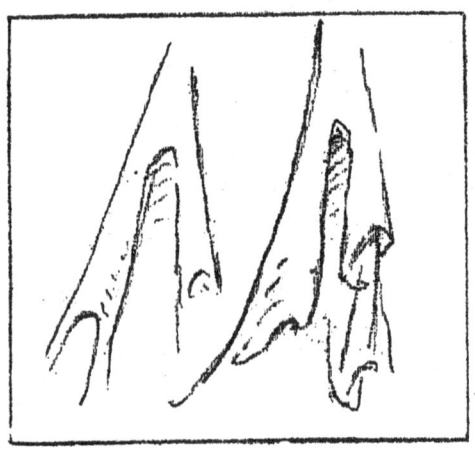

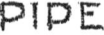

PIPE

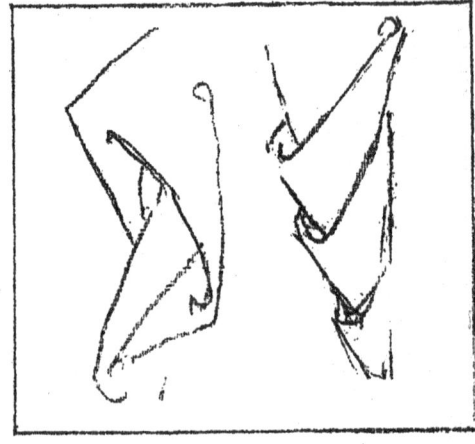

ZIGZAG

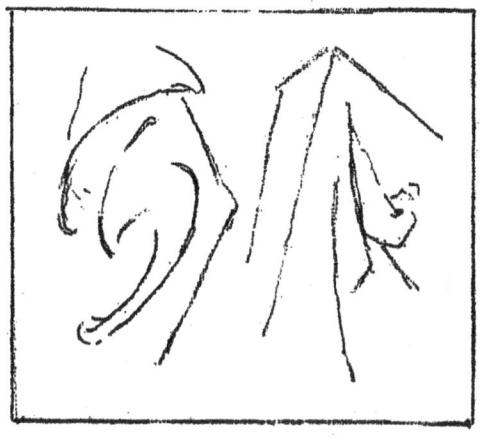

SPIRAL

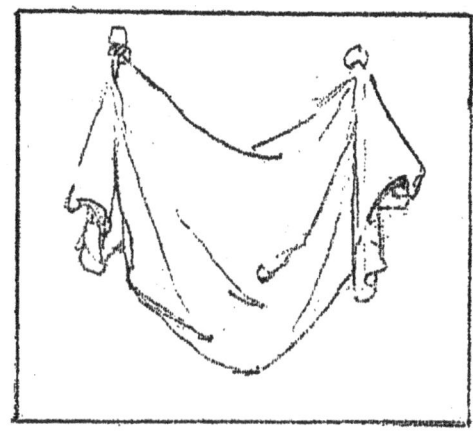

DIAPER

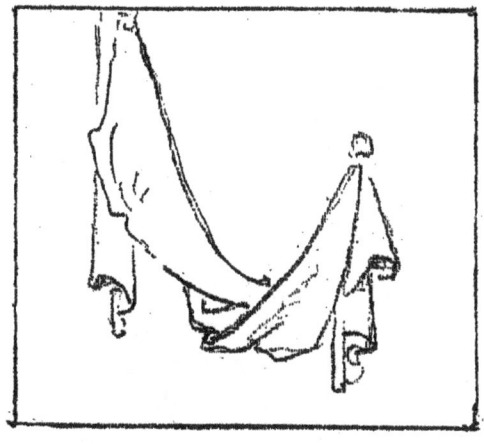

HALF LOCK

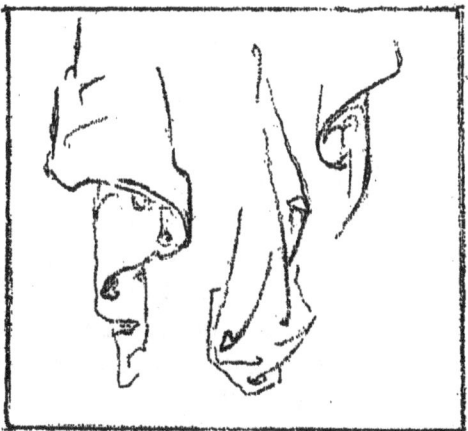

DROP

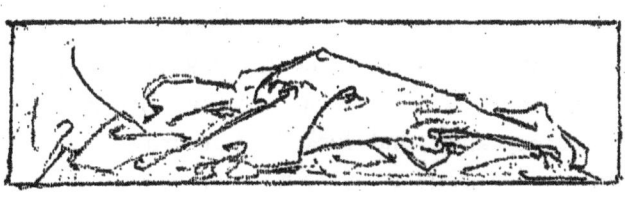

INERT

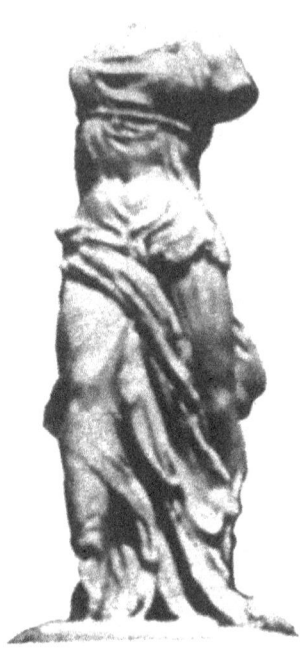

## DRAPERY

DRESS materials in themselves have no form. When lying on the floor they conform to the floor; thrown over a chair they take the contour of the chair on which they rest; if on a hanger or hook, the folds descend from their support. Drapery therefore, is nothing definite in itself as it depends entirely upon that which lies beneath. Drapery may encircle, it may fall or it may be drawn upward. To realize this is the first step to the understanding of drapery. There is no sameness, no monotony, every fold has a distinct character of its own. To show this vast difference in folds take the figure of Victory as an example. First, the diaper pattern which in this case falls from its fixed points of support at the shoulders is the simplest of all folds to understand. Next, a spiral fold is drawn around the receding hips; opposed to this spiral is a fold of a totally different character. It is irregular and zigzags from side to side. Below this another distinct type of fold appears, known as the pipe or cord fold. Beneath this another type emerges, called a half-lock. This in turn shares its form with that which lies prone upon the floor and is known by the name, inert. There is also the fold that is carried away from the body by its movement or by the air and is known as the drop fold or a piece of flying drapery.

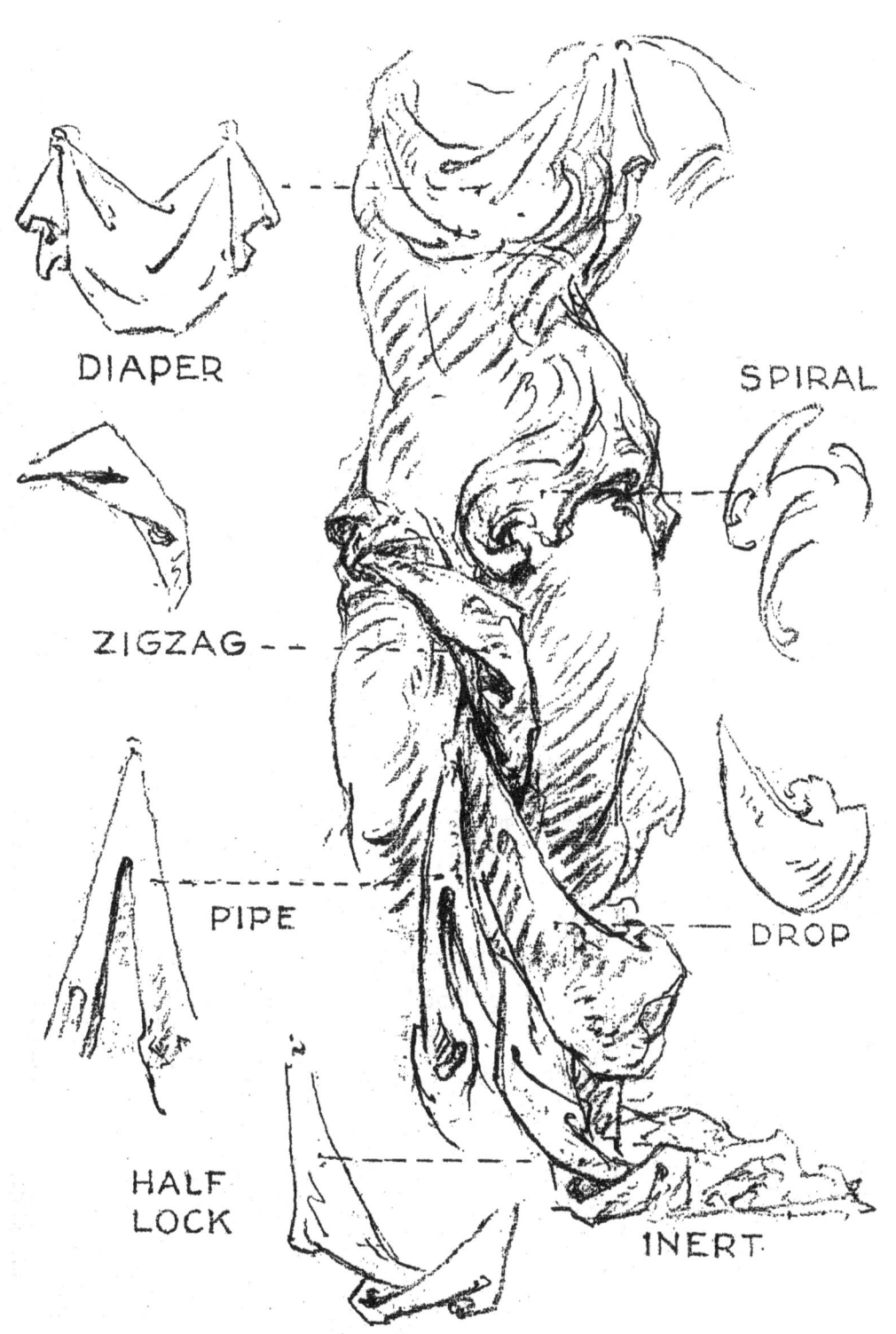

DIAPER

SPIRAL

ZIGZAG

PIPE

DROP

HALF
LOCK

INERT

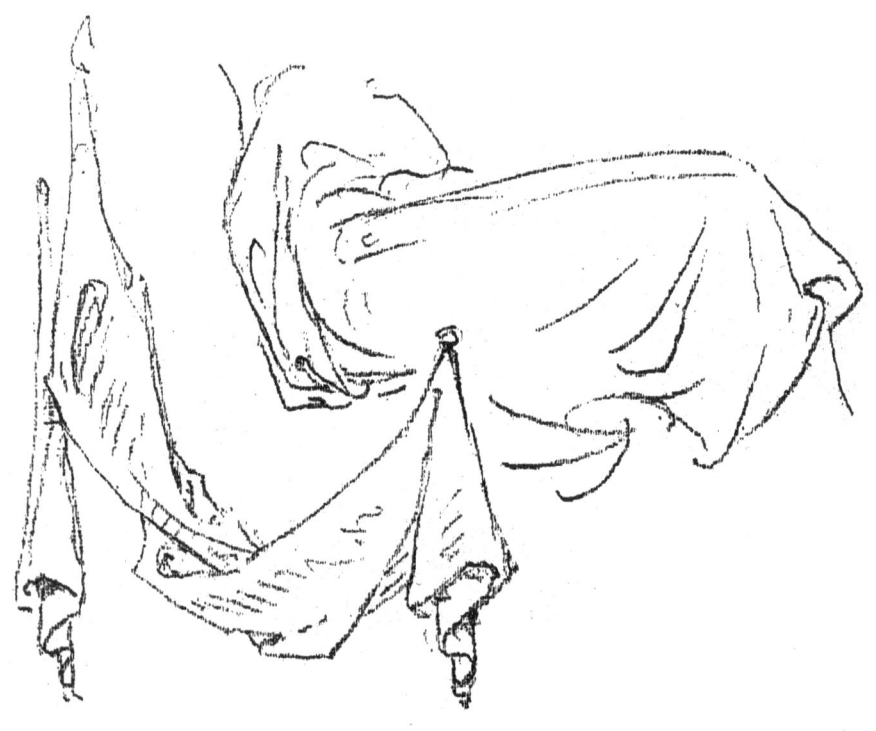

## THE DIFFERENT CHARACTERS
## OF FOLDS

Each fold has a character of its own. If but one formation was used, the design would be monotonous and insipid. If drapery is drawn upward it causes one kind of fold; if allowed to fall, another form of fold is created. Folds passing from one point of support to another make distinct arrangements such as zigzags and half-locks, while others as they meet, die away and are known as the diaper pattern. One is angular in formation, the other spiral or rhythmic. The formation of folds must be recognized as a law, as folds are of such complex character it is difficult to observe these facts.

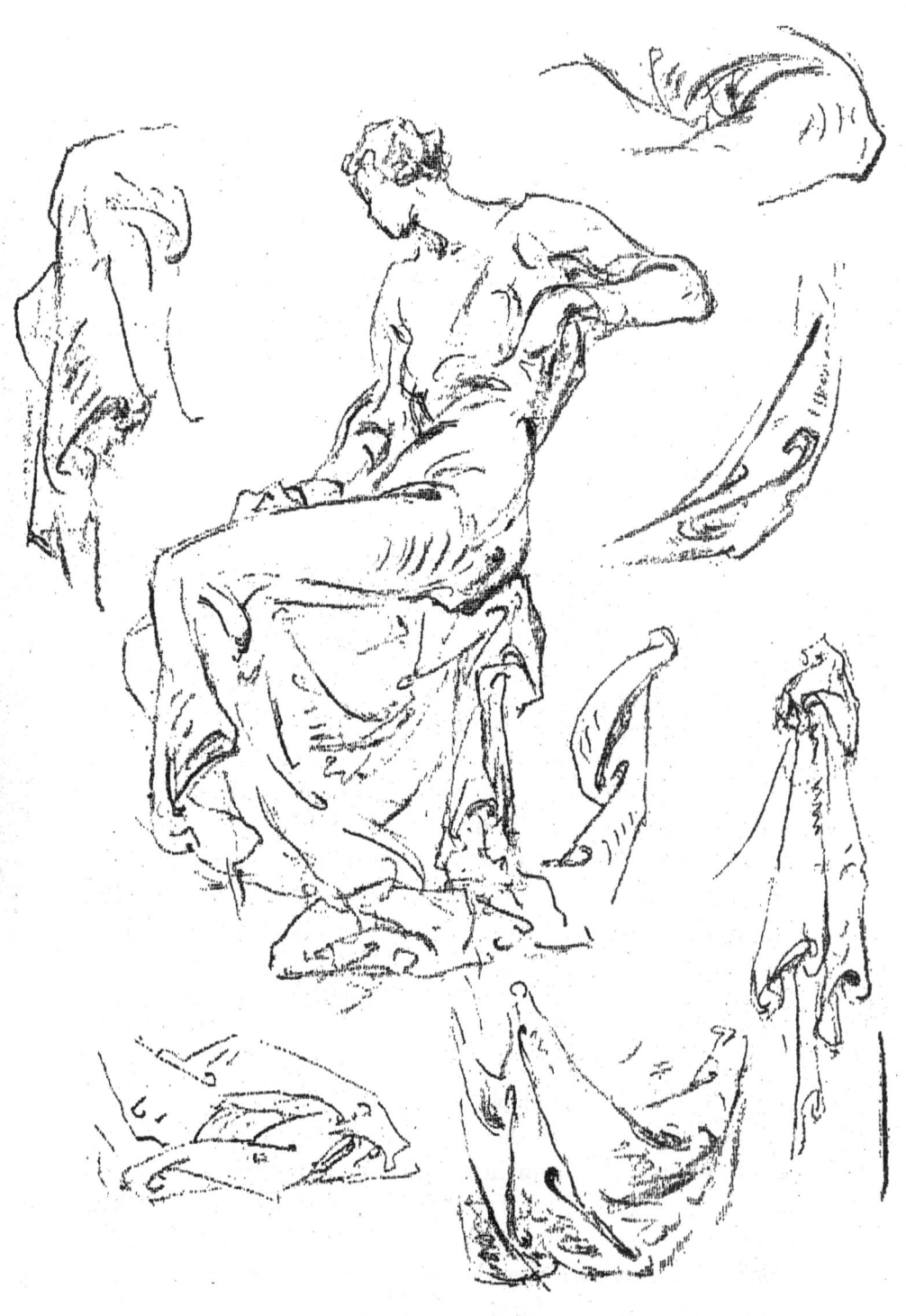

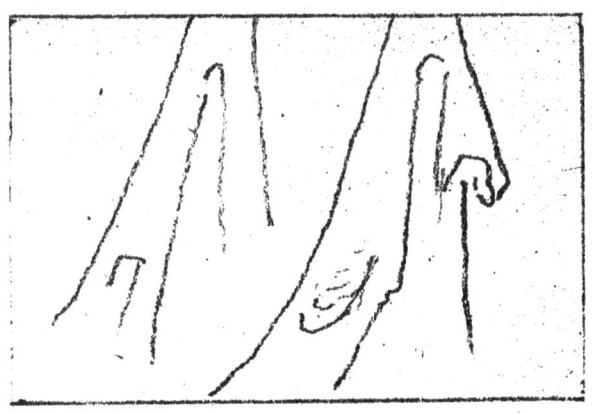

## PIPE OR DROP FOLDS

IF A piece of cloth is held up or nailed by one corner and then pulled from the other corner, tubular forms radiate from its fixed point. Whether the cloth is woolen, cotton or silk; whether it is thick, thin, old or new, the same radiation, the same tube or pipe-like forms are always prevalent. This is a distinct fact, therefore it must be recognized as a law as it is something that repeats itself often enough to be recognized as such, something to look for, something you expect to find.

These radiating cords or summits as they descend from their points of support are the simplest forms in drapery and are the first to be understood. A simple cord fold will descend and then divide into two or three other cords. As these diverge from each other, the original cords may make room for two or more within them, then these may again divide, making two or more until they flatten out. The breaking out and divergence of these primary folds is simple but of extreme importance. The pull as well as the force of the pull must be understood. This thought makes the drawing understandable to the observer. Radiating lines should not be abused but should be studied carefully. These laws may be studied apart from the model, but it requires a draped figure for verification. Then if the folds take different form, it will be found that these pipes or cords of drapery radiate from the points of support until they clasp the exposed parts of the figure where they cling to the form beneath.

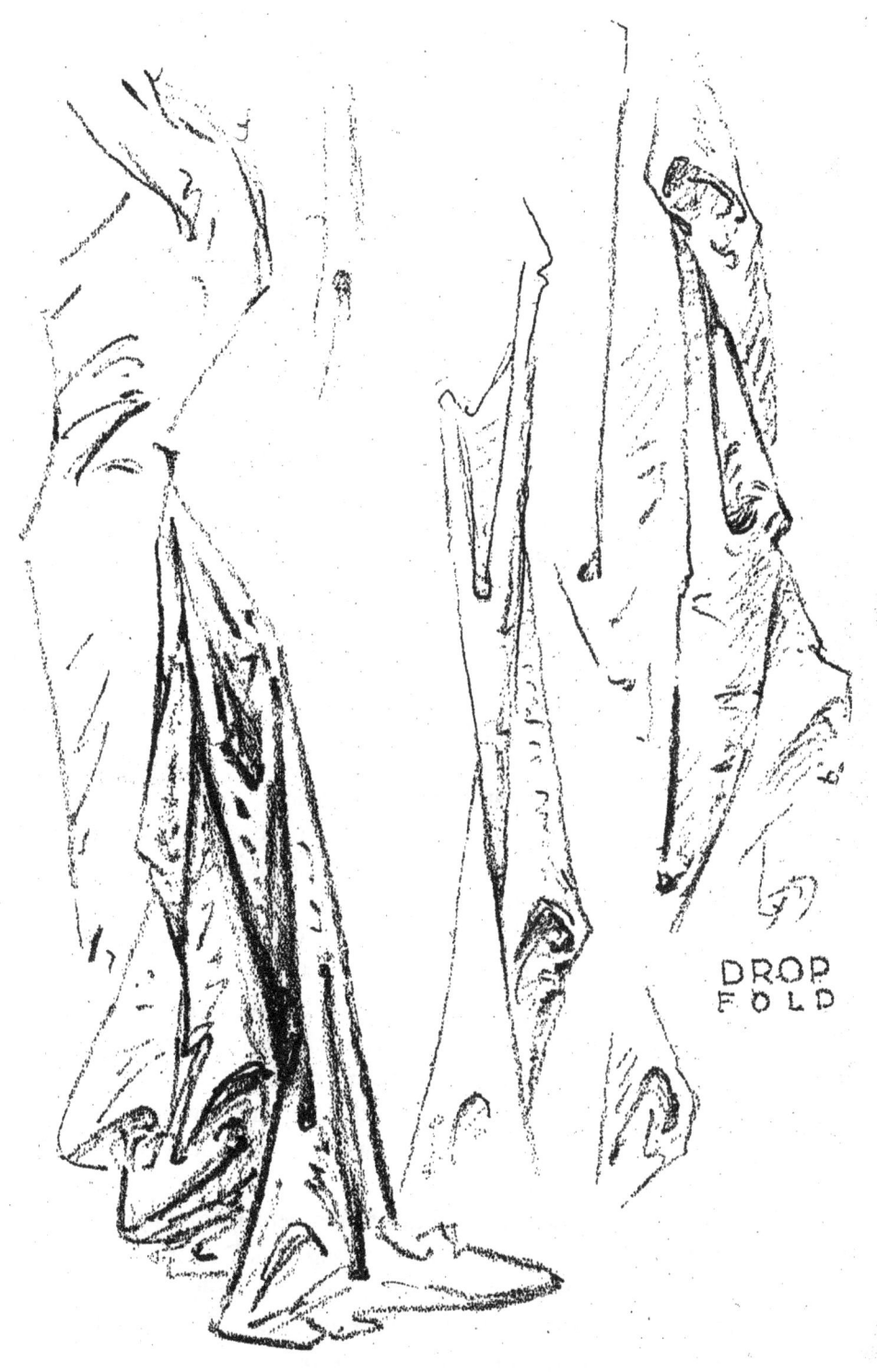

DROP
FOLD

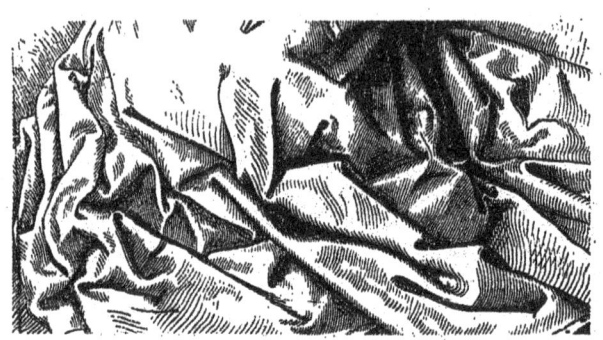

## ZIGZAG FOLDS

A TUBULAR fold of cloth may be bent. As it bends the outer portion becomes rigid and underneath becomes more slack. This excess cloth on the inner side buckles into a more or less definite pattern which must be figured out and remembered. The twisting of this fold when bent gives an entirely new design, one which might be called a zigzag pattern.

Here the pull is uneven in character. It is quick and jerky. To demonstrate this, take six single sheets of newspaper, roll them into a two inch cylinder, bend the roll in the middle, now grasp the roll near each side of the bend and give it a sharp twist from side to side. Note the pattern and the design. You can reason out why these bendings and twistings so consistently repeat themselves. Try it out on a piece of stiff cloth and you will find a familiar resemblance. It is this repetition that must be stored away in your mind so that you may check your knowledge with what you see on the model. Remember at all times that each fold has a character apart from every other fold; remember that you will have a preference as to folds; that some folds will appeal to you more than others, making your drawings different from other drawings. Remember that the things you know and leave out, are the things that give the power and simplicity to your drawings.

Students gain much by making a number of drawings that will tell the story of an interlocking zigzag fold. Do not copy the drawings on the opposite page, start with a straight or curved line and try to lock the ends with other lines that will account for the bringing together the two opposing forces.

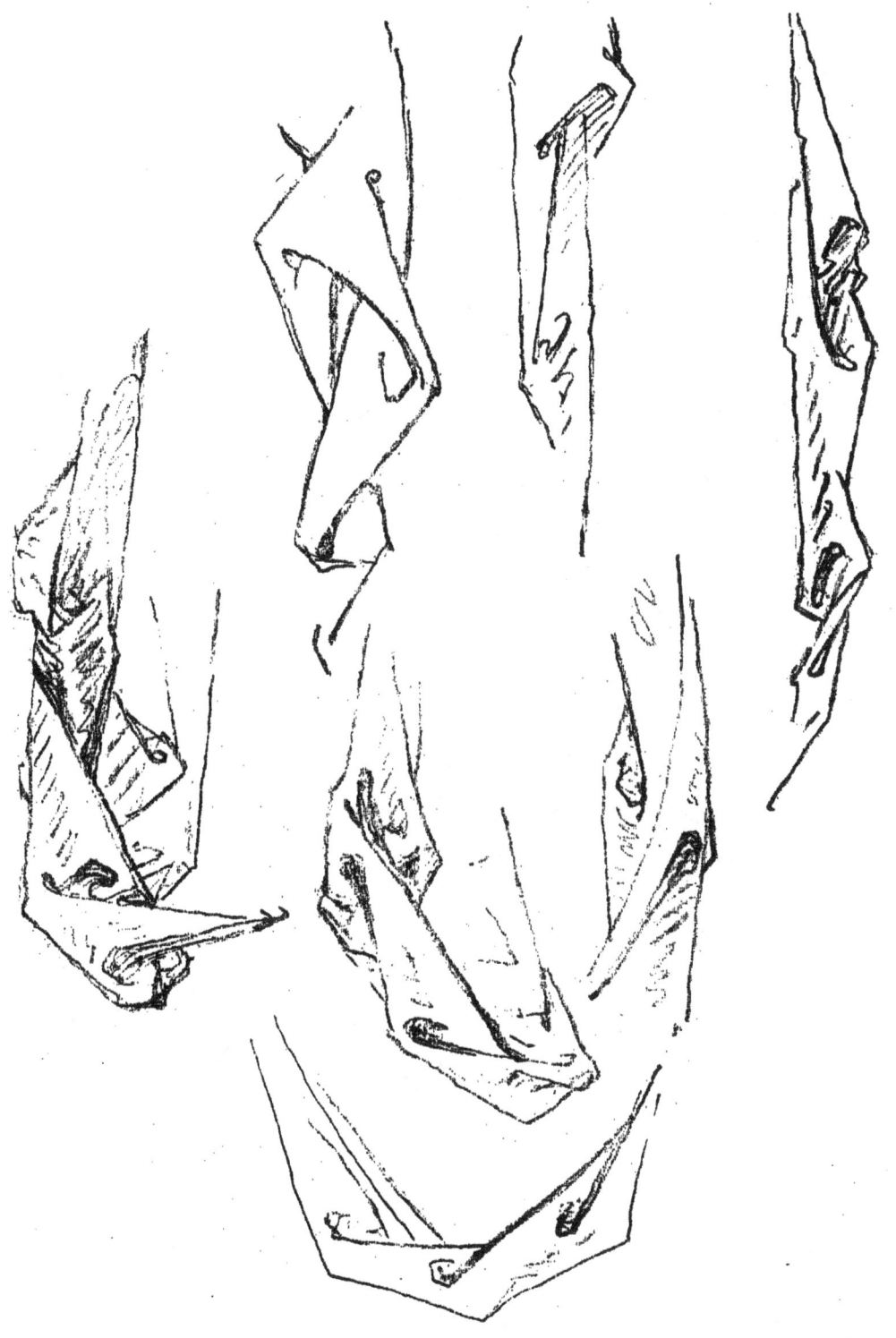

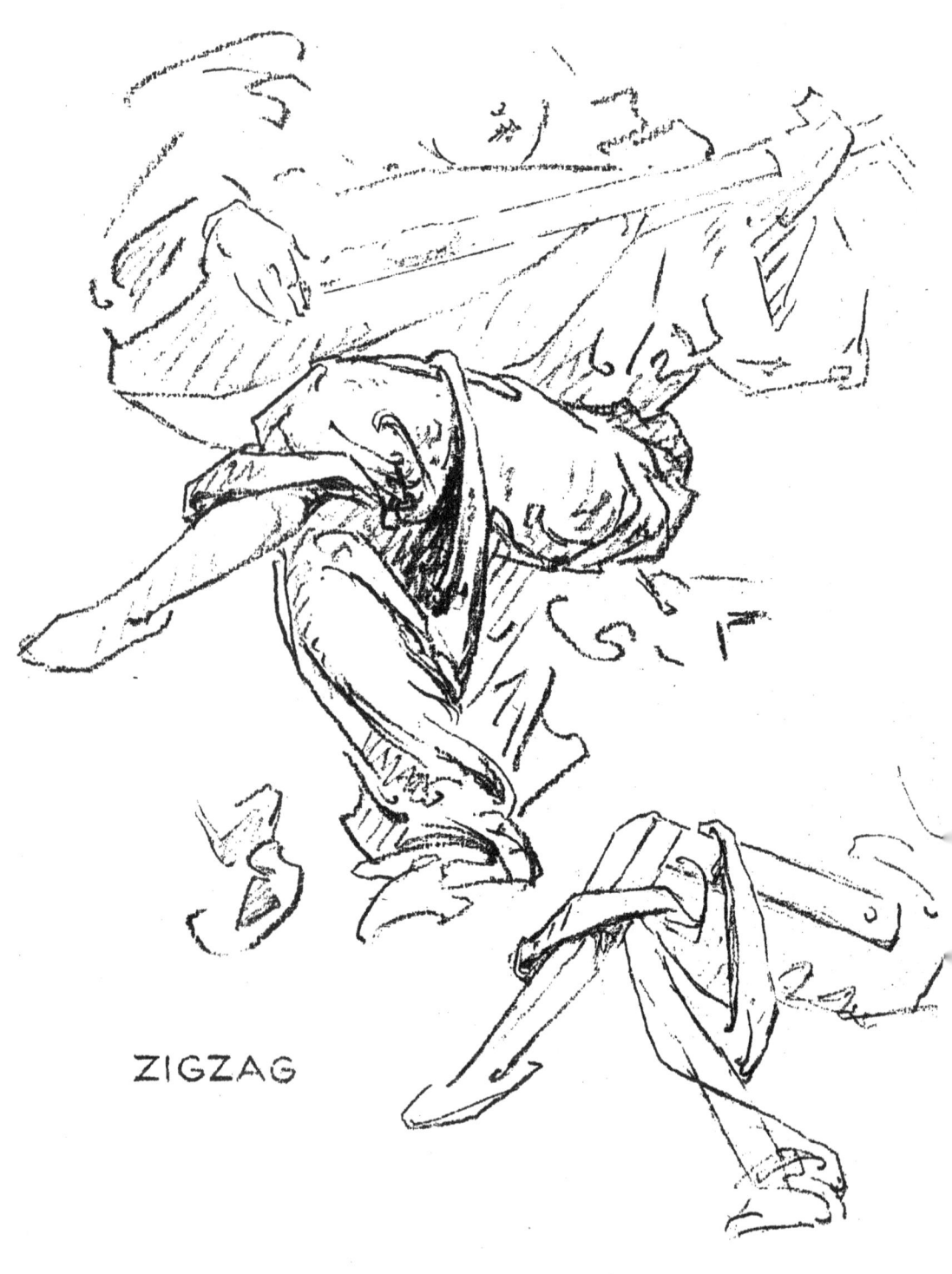

ZIGZAG

CARPACCIO

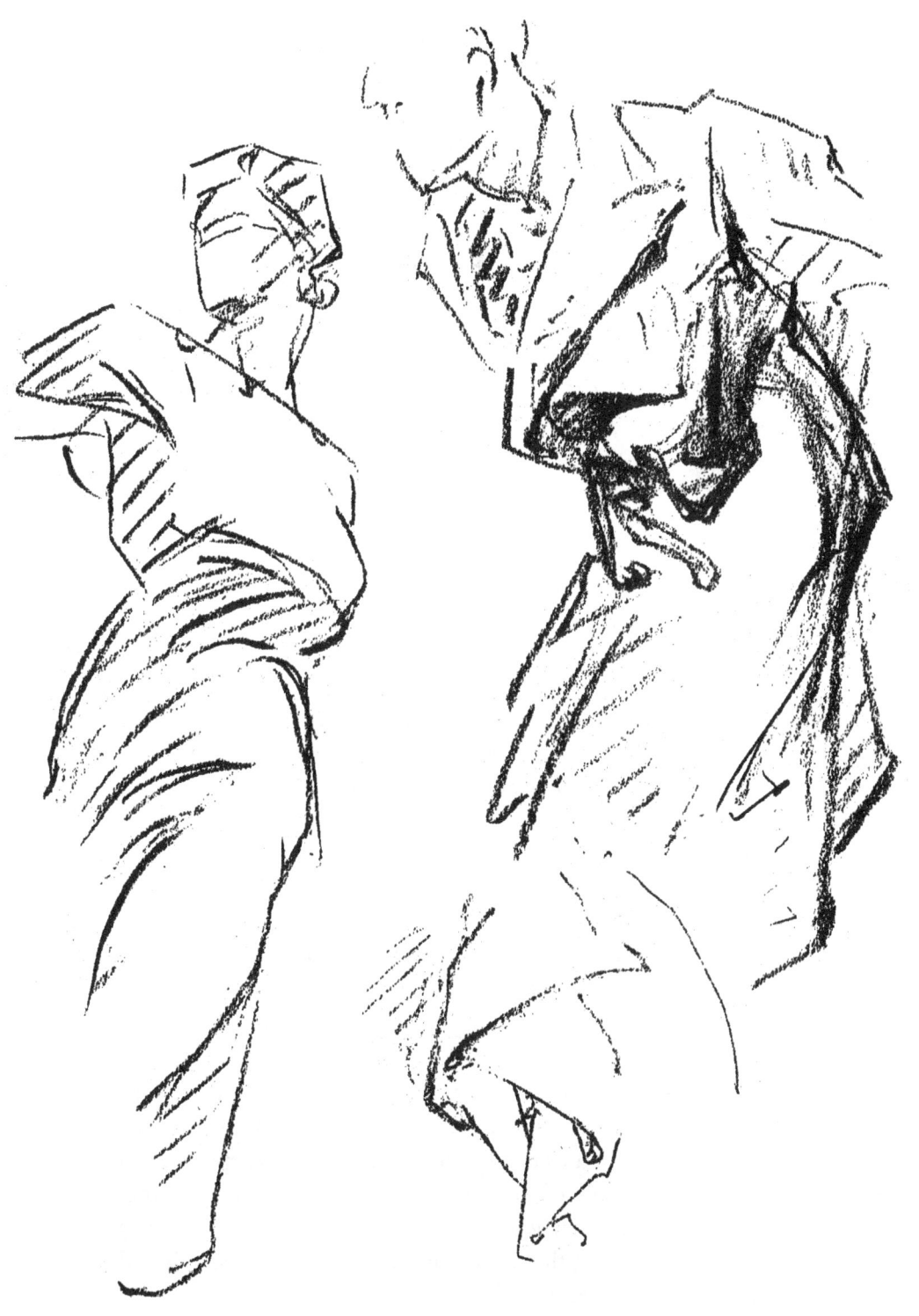

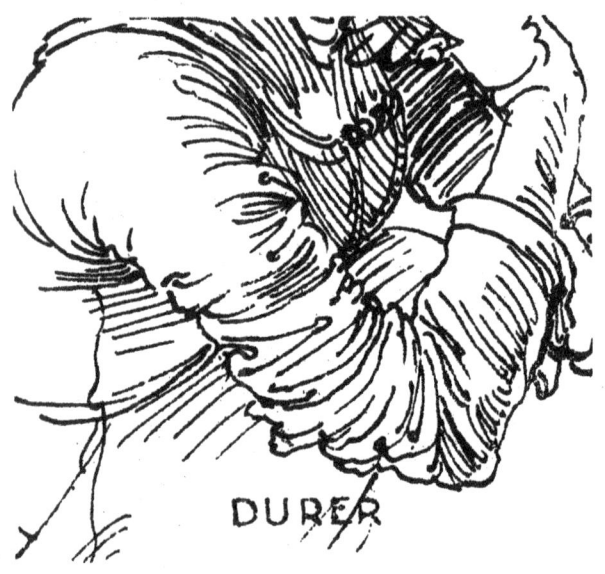

DURER

## SPIRAL

No MATTER how complicated the fold appears, it can be traced to a few basic principles. These few principles should be catalogued and kept as far apart in the mind as possible. One should be able to draw at all times, any one of these seven distinctive characters without notes or a model. Think of the part they play so that when confronted by the costumed model, you are less liable to get lost in depicting these ever changing folds. The arrangement of curved and diagonal lines fit the rounded forms of the body as the material wraps around the figure. In the same manner folds widen as they leave their points of support. It is safe to say as they radiate away from the point of support they seldom parallel. To a great extent, these radiating folds should have a decorative arrangement as well as an understanding; (the knowledge that there is the art of knowing what to leave out). As a sleeve enters the shoulders, the design calls for both curved and straight lines. Where the elbow is bent, the material radiates outward and up to encircle the wedge that occurs on the outer side of the forearm just above the elbow. The number of folds depend upon the texture or weight of the fabric as well as the number of times the garment has been worn. Folds should not look as if they paralleled nor repeat themselves in direction or volume, with all an understanding sense of design and pattern.

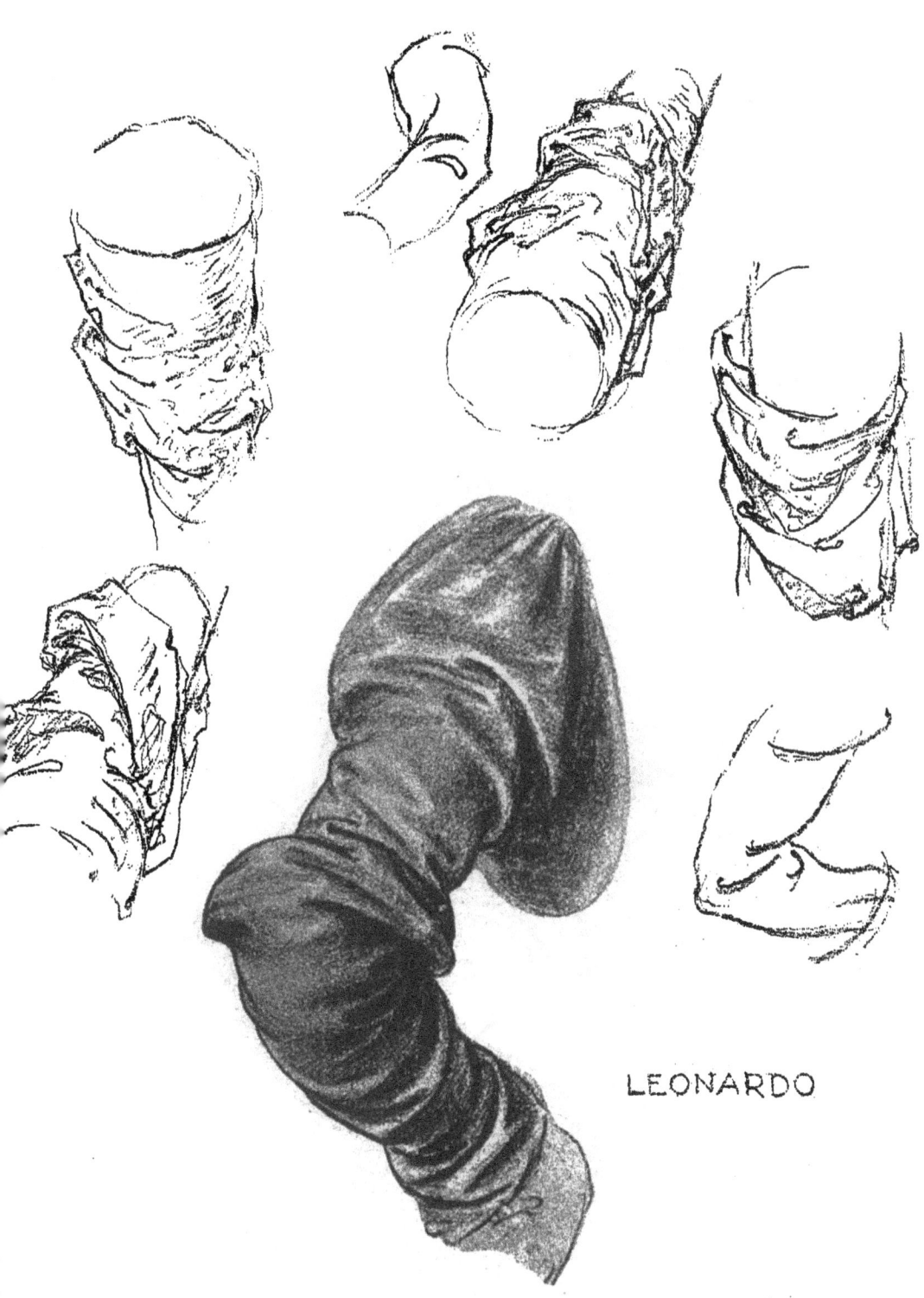

LEONARDO

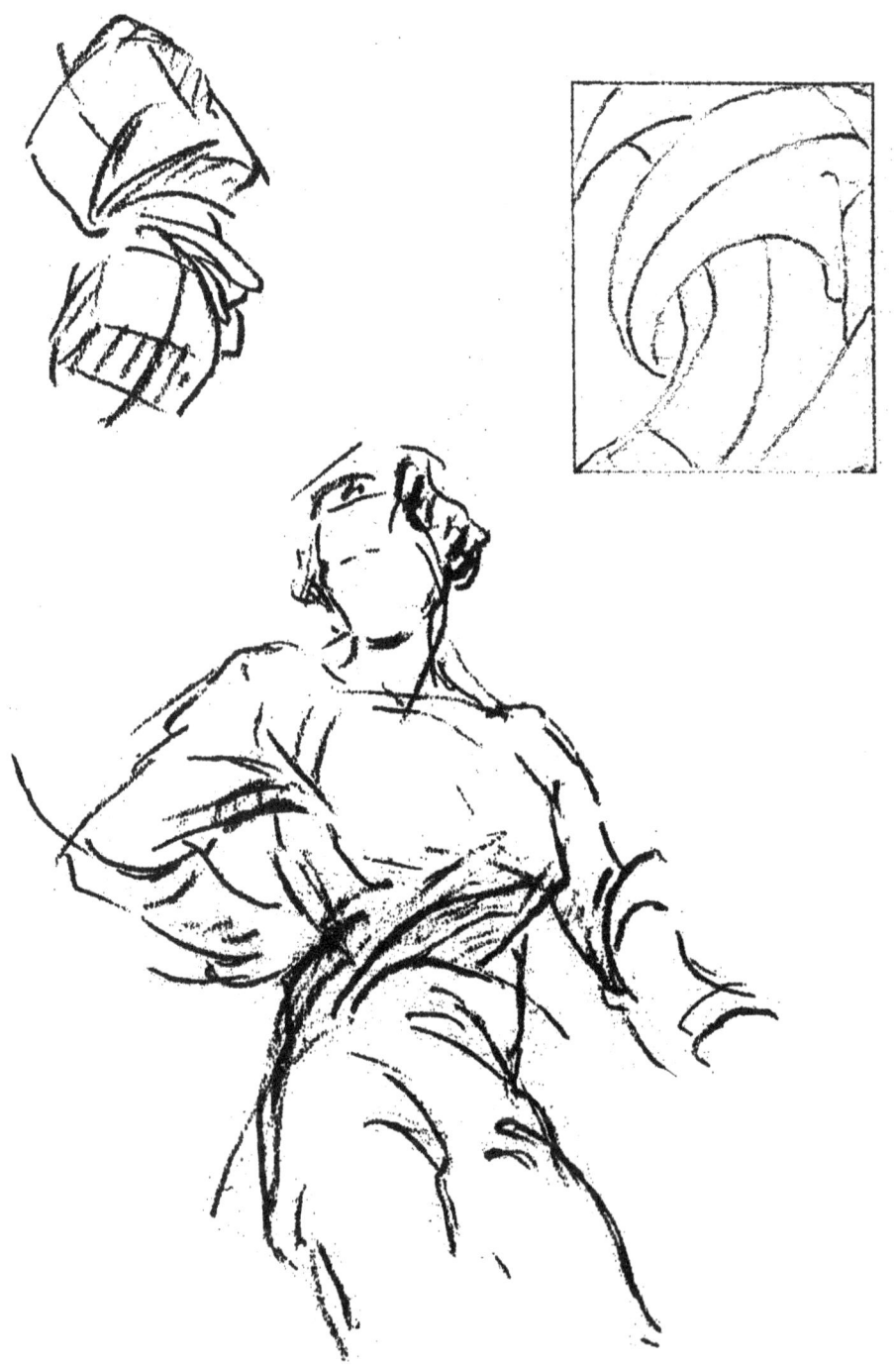

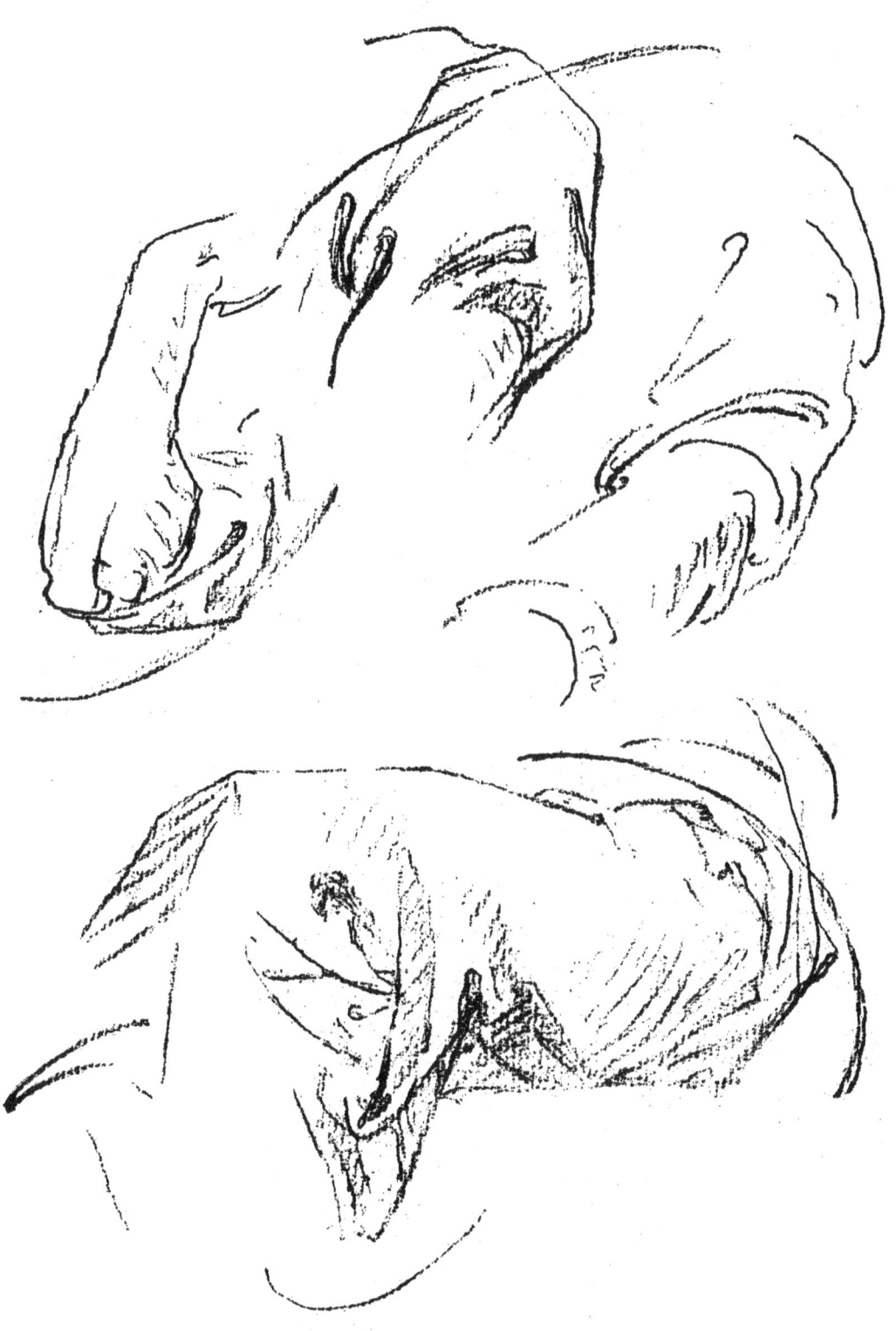

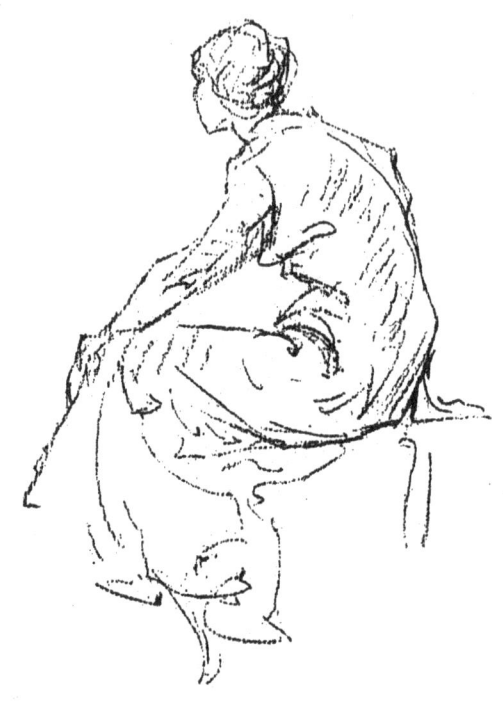

# ARRANGEMENT

THE design of a draped figure must first be good in proportion and each portion be relevant to the whole. The detail must have a relation to the main design and not be plastered over with meaningless zigzags and sagging folds that do not contribute to the real form of the body which must be preserved and not broken up my minute detail. To arrange these details comes under the head of composition. In composition there must be rhythm, charm, and if the subject calls for it even beauty, a word for which no one can give a satisfactory definition, yet all this enters into a composition. The draped figure must be a complete pattern in itself.

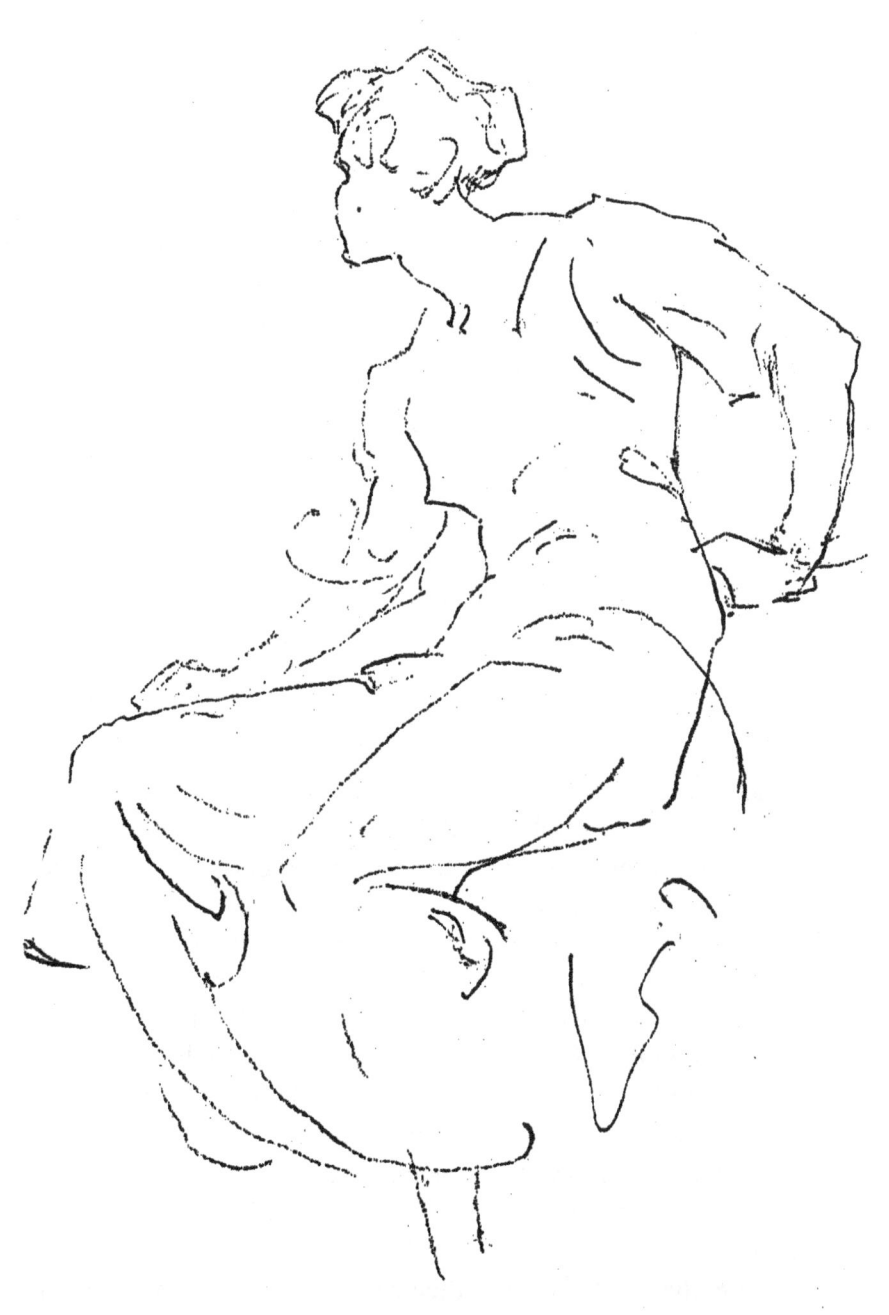

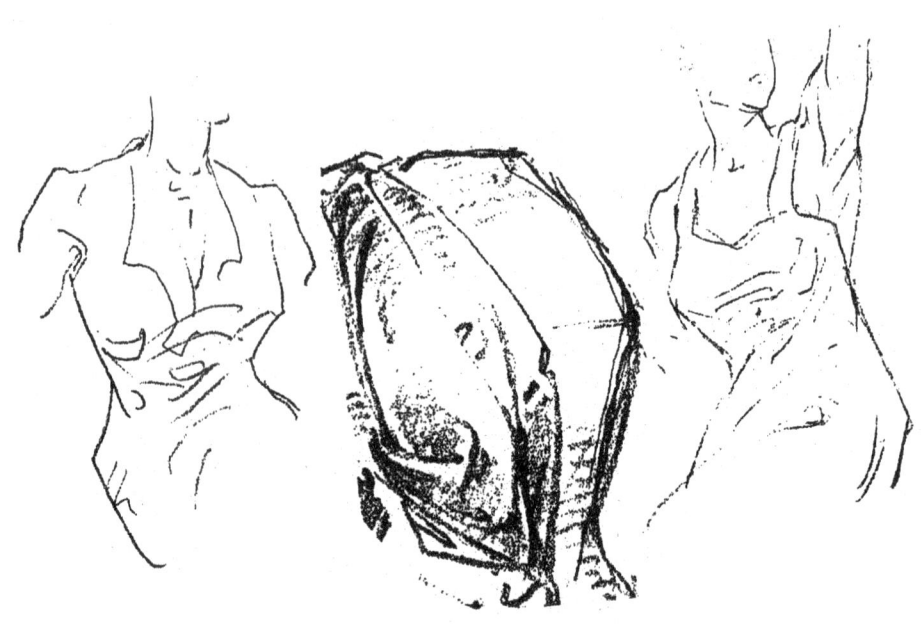

## DIAPER PATTERN

THE material that drapes a figure has no form nor shape. It is the change of form under the material that gives a reason for the different character that a fold takes. Every fold must have its support. It either pulls or is being pulled; it clings or it folds; it encircles or it is festooned, but in every case it must be supported. It does not become drapery until it is supported by something. Take a yard or so of plain material in both hands; hold it by the two upper corners and allow the center to sag. It shows how the folds festoon and lock into each other toward the center. Try both light and heavy materials until you note the relationship in the radiating lines. Trace the fold or crease from the point of support by which it is being held. Follow to where the two sagging opposing forces meet and study carefully how they interlock. Still holding the two corners at arms length bring the ends nearer together and note the changes that take place and in the way they repeat themselves. After you have the idea as to how the festoon locks, the goods may be thumb-tacked to a board or to the wall or placed on a lay figure. On the latter, arrange the goods first and then turn the figure in the position desired. Thus through observation you gain the construction and sense of another fold that is distinct in character from any other fold, and has been known for centuries as the Diaper Pattern.

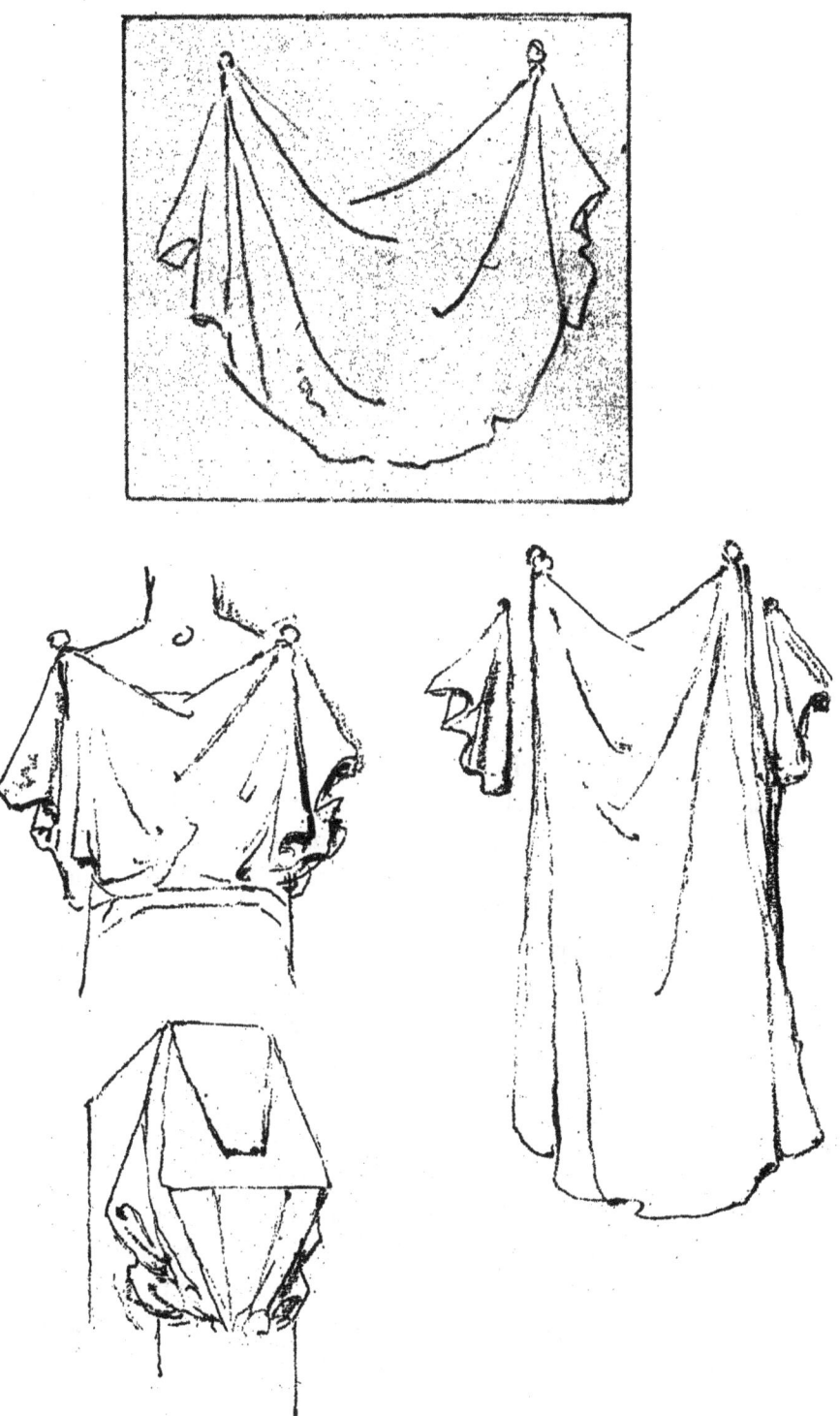

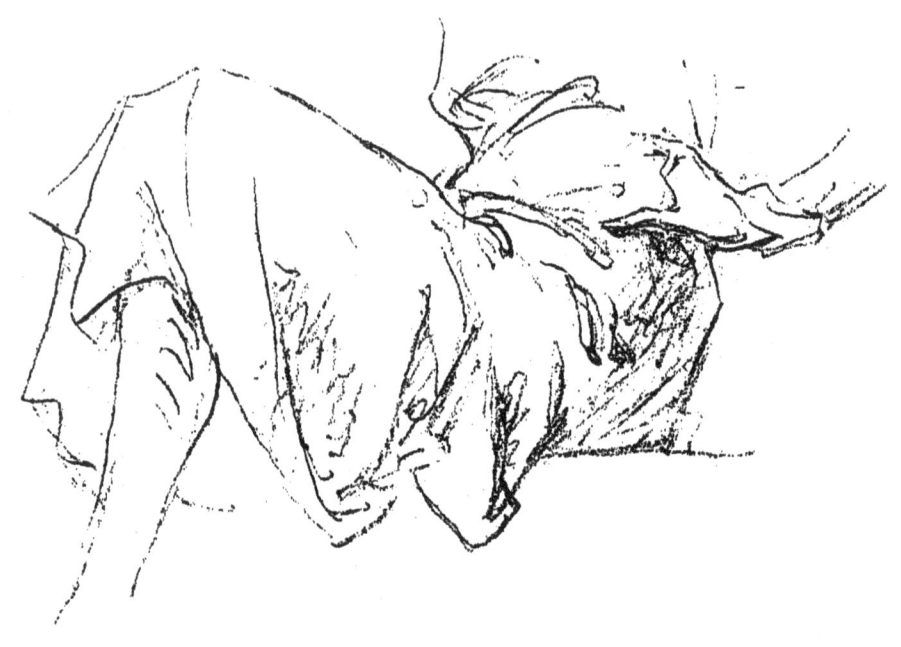

## HALF-LOCK FOLD

THE half-lock takes place every time a tubular or flattened piece of material abruptly changes its direction. When the turn is at or near a right angle, the locking is more sharp and angular; when they fall in sweeping curves, the locks are more rounded and are apt to dissolve one into the other. Folds must be made to explain themselves without difficulty, therefore, must be direct and simple. Each fold must appear to be as far apart in character as the letters of the alphabet and as letters when brought together to form a word. As each letter seems to dissolve itself into that word and that again into a sentence, so it is with folds, each with a distinct character, yet when brought together the pipe, zigzag, spiral, half-lock, diaper, festoon and drop folds must dissolve one into the other making one harmonious element called the draped figure. Each has its own function. Each is supported from or by the form underneath. The half-lock is more prevalent in a sitting down figure due to the greater number of angles causing a greater change in the direction of planes.

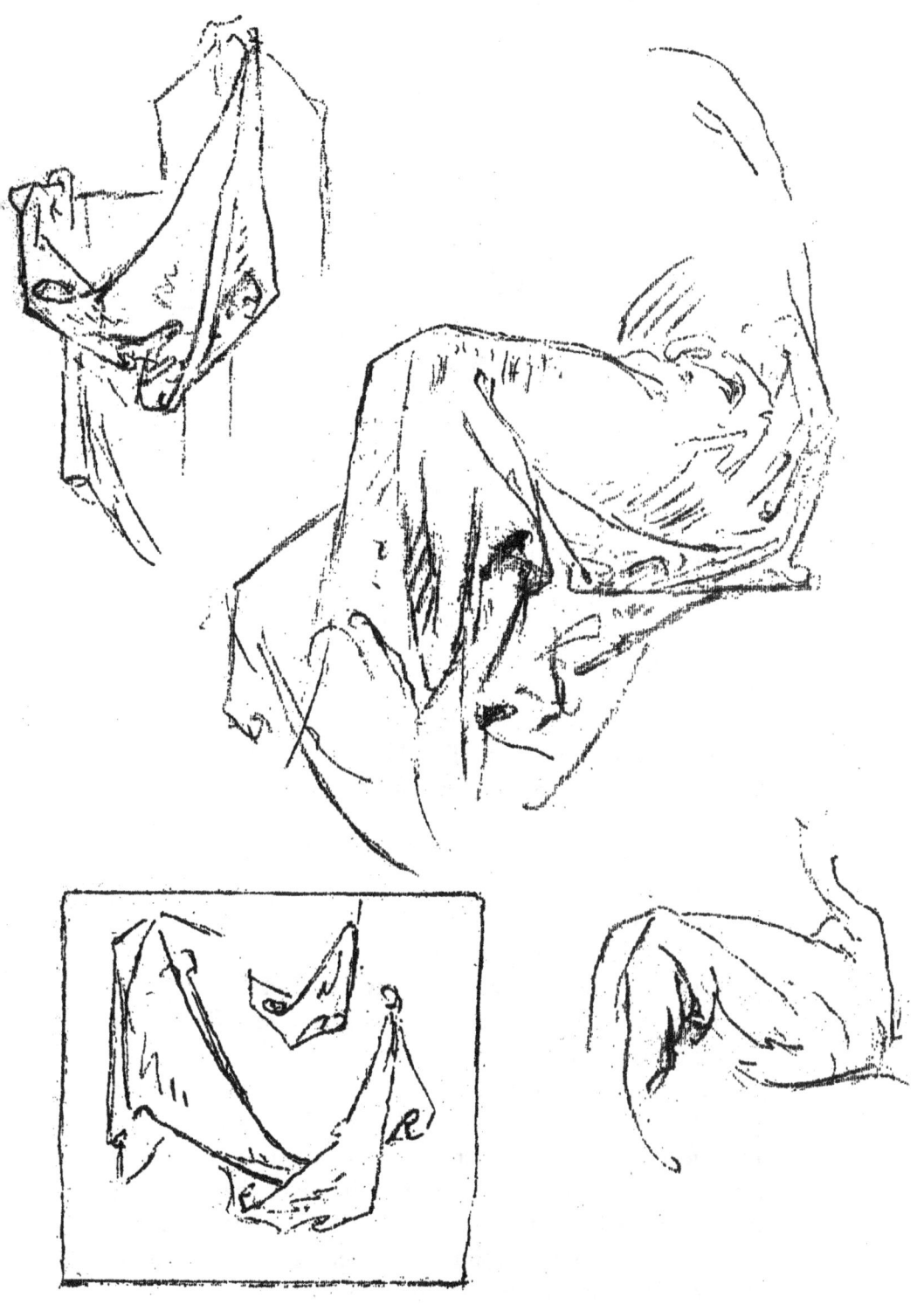

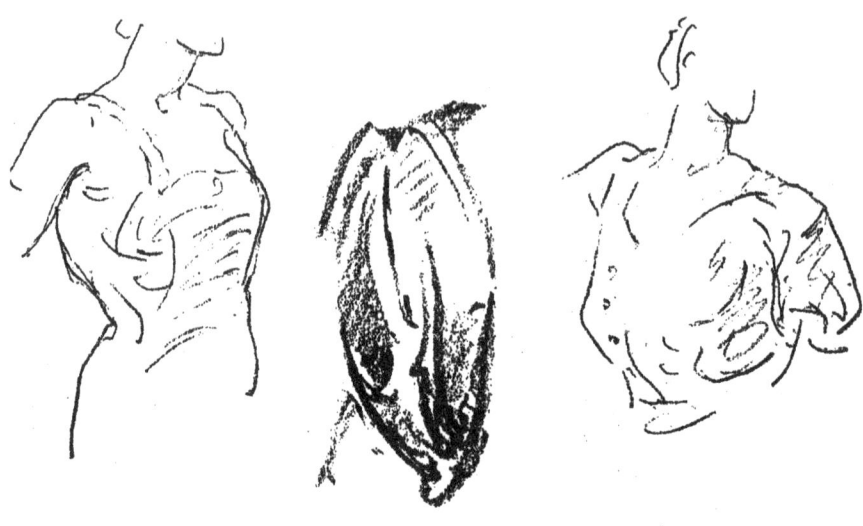

## DIAPER

Hold the material at arms' length, drop one corner and it will be seen that the radiations are longer and of greater volume on the side that is held high and that it locks in a more abrupt manner on the lower side. Again bring the material to a horizontal line and it will be found that the system of radiating lines and their locking into one another is less complicated than when the opposing forces are not equal. The shifting of these two points of support must be studied and brought to some basic form that is understandable.

Do not think of drapery as a piece of still life; try to get at the facts and when the facts are known, then it is a matter of good judgment. This when summed up, means the art of knowing what to leave out, putting in only the important things that give the character of each separate and individual fold. Remember to keep their characters as far apart as possible for each fold has its own mission and duty.

Folds when they turn at an angle either intersect or lock into each other in the form of a hook or break. When they turn, and take a gentle curve, they flatten out to broader areas. As the fold turns, it is the kind that is formed at the break that has to be carefully studied in detail. The crispness or the softness of the material is the only variation of a fold that is bent, the general structure of the material remains the same.

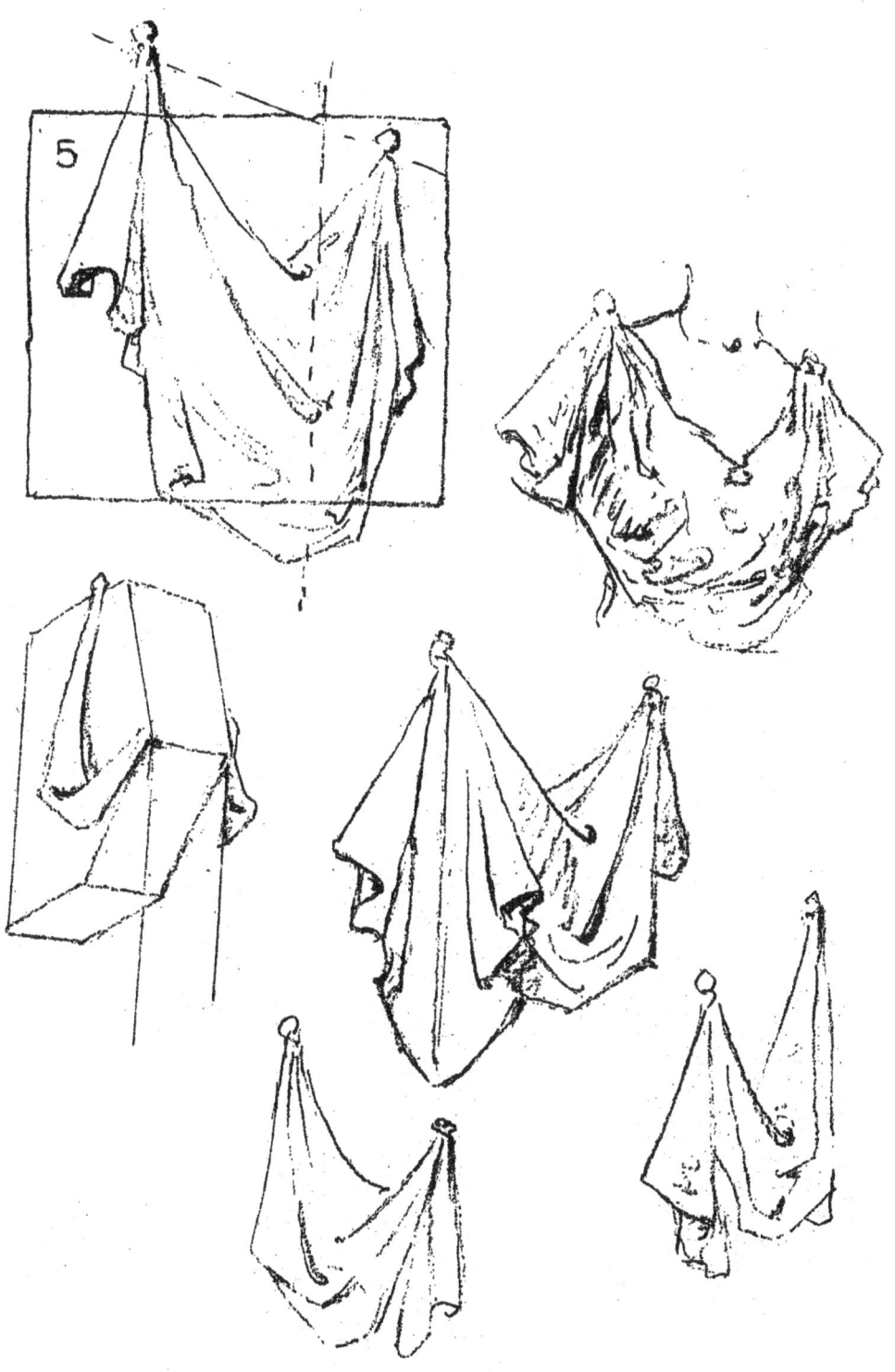

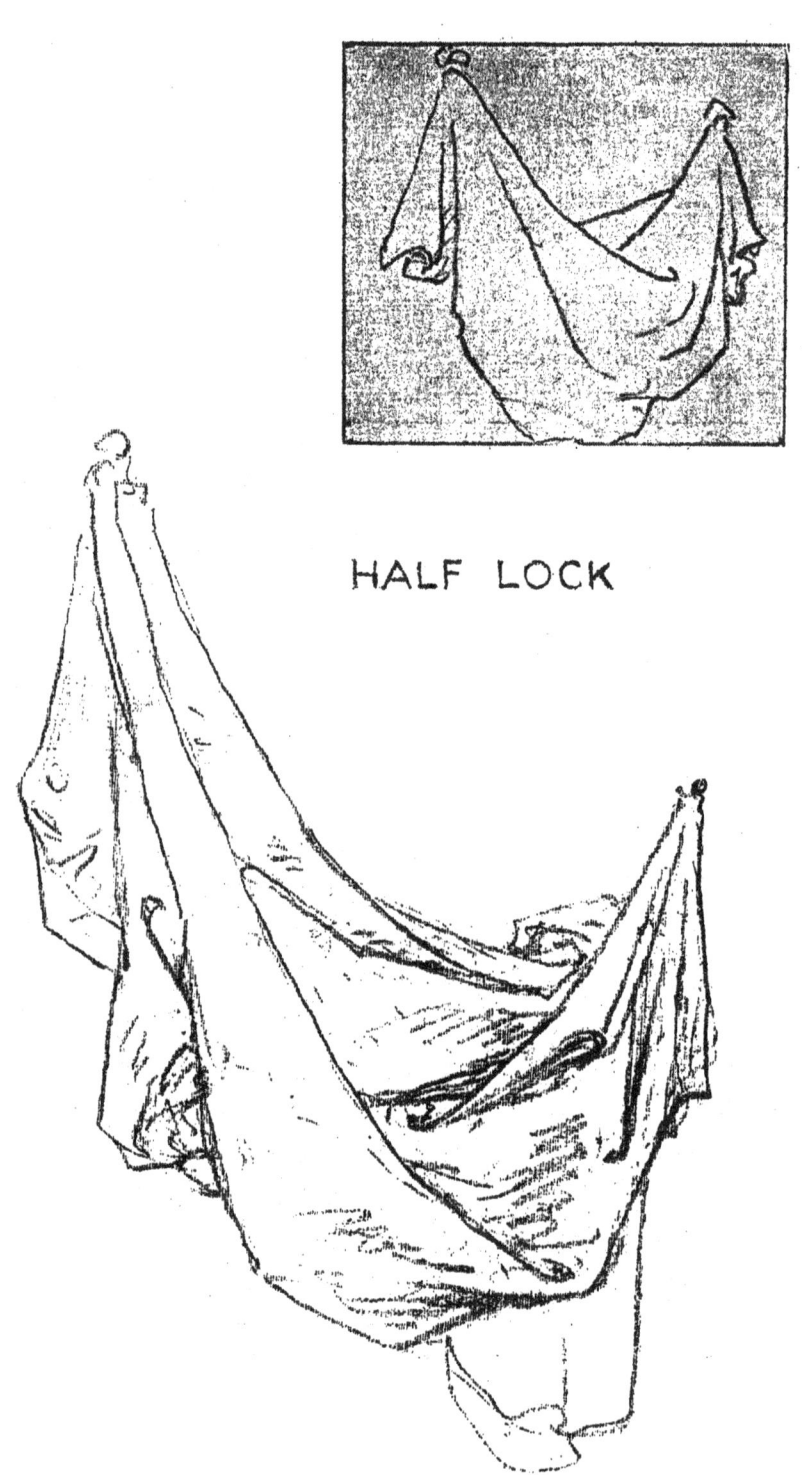

HALF LOCK

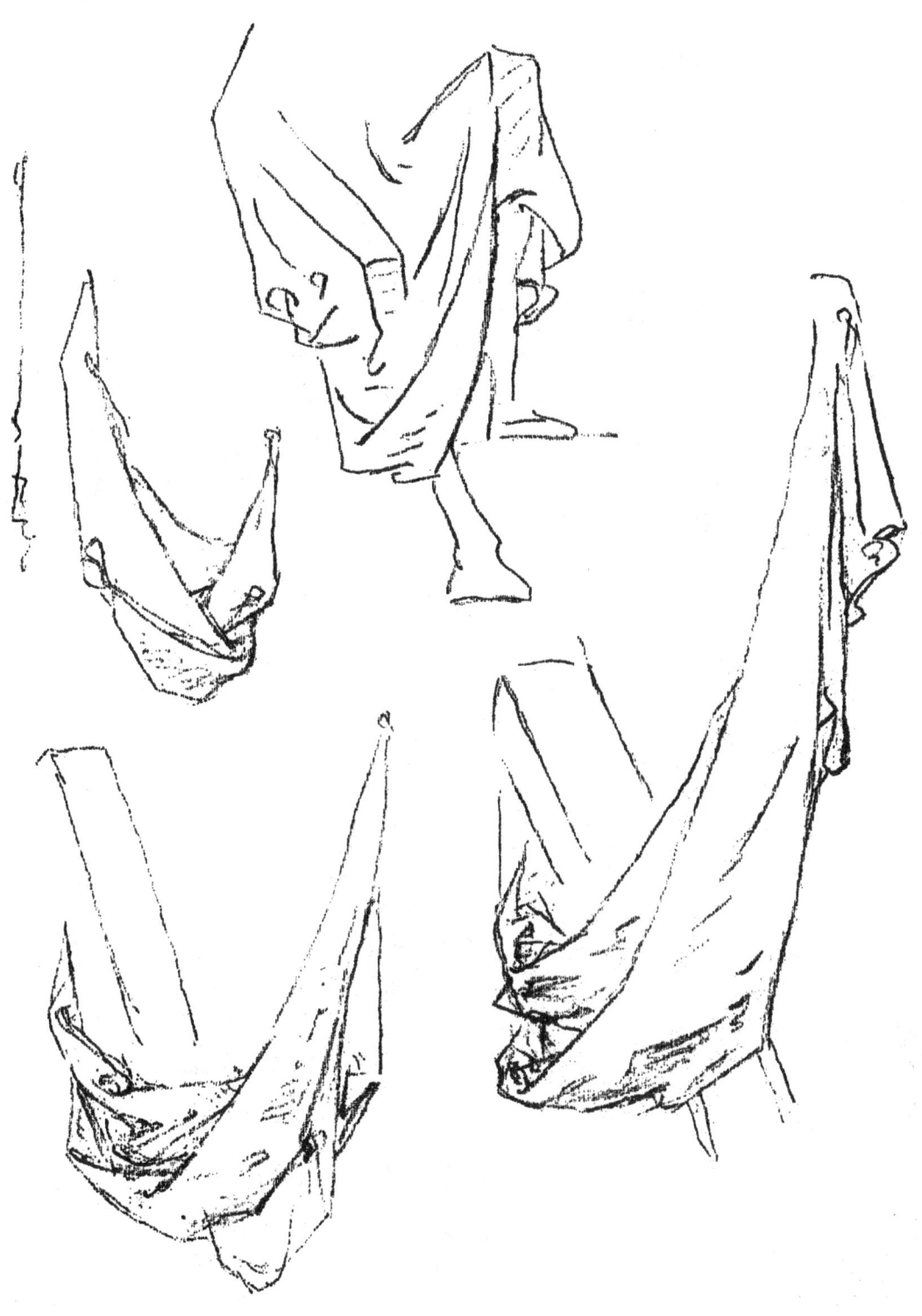

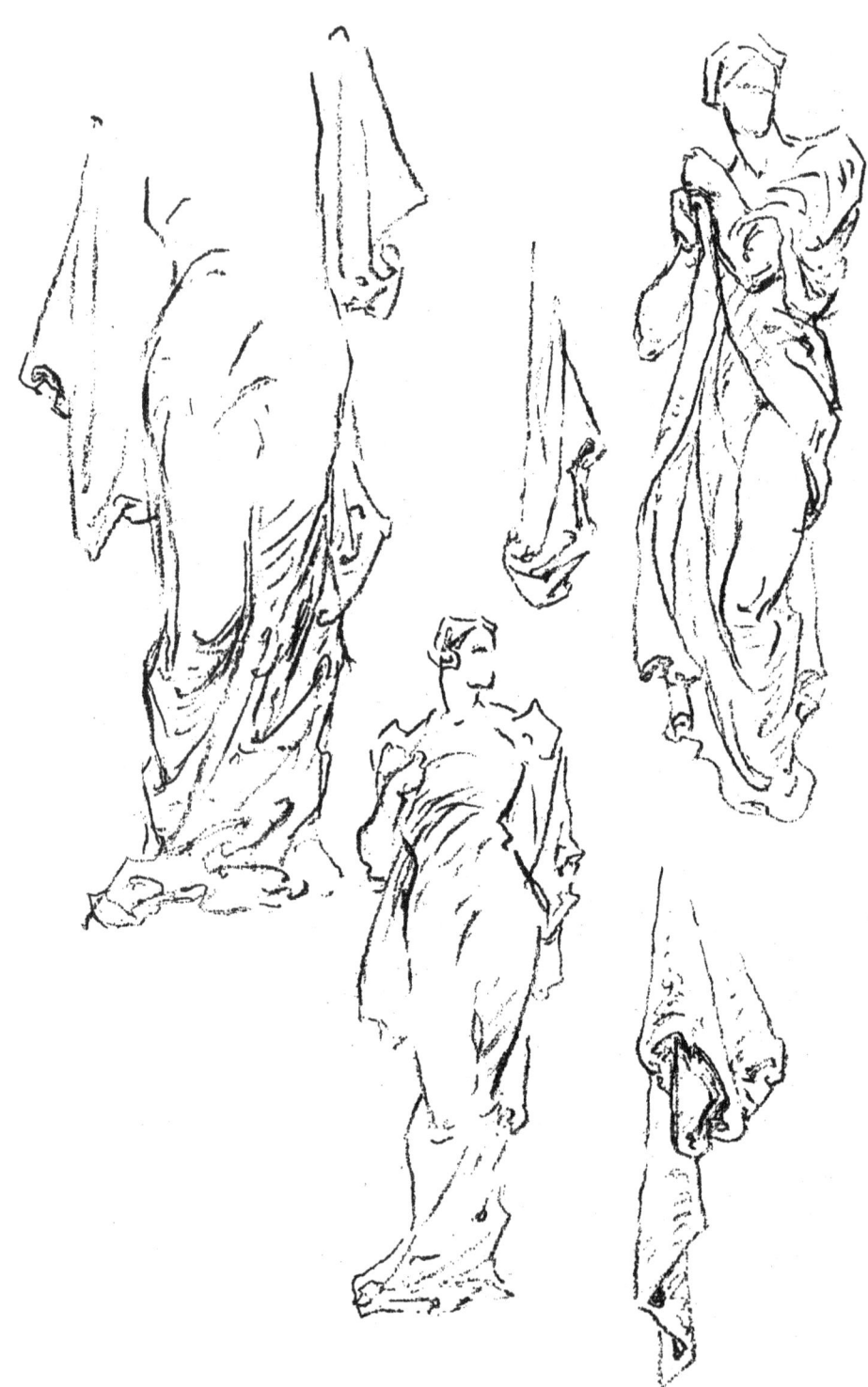

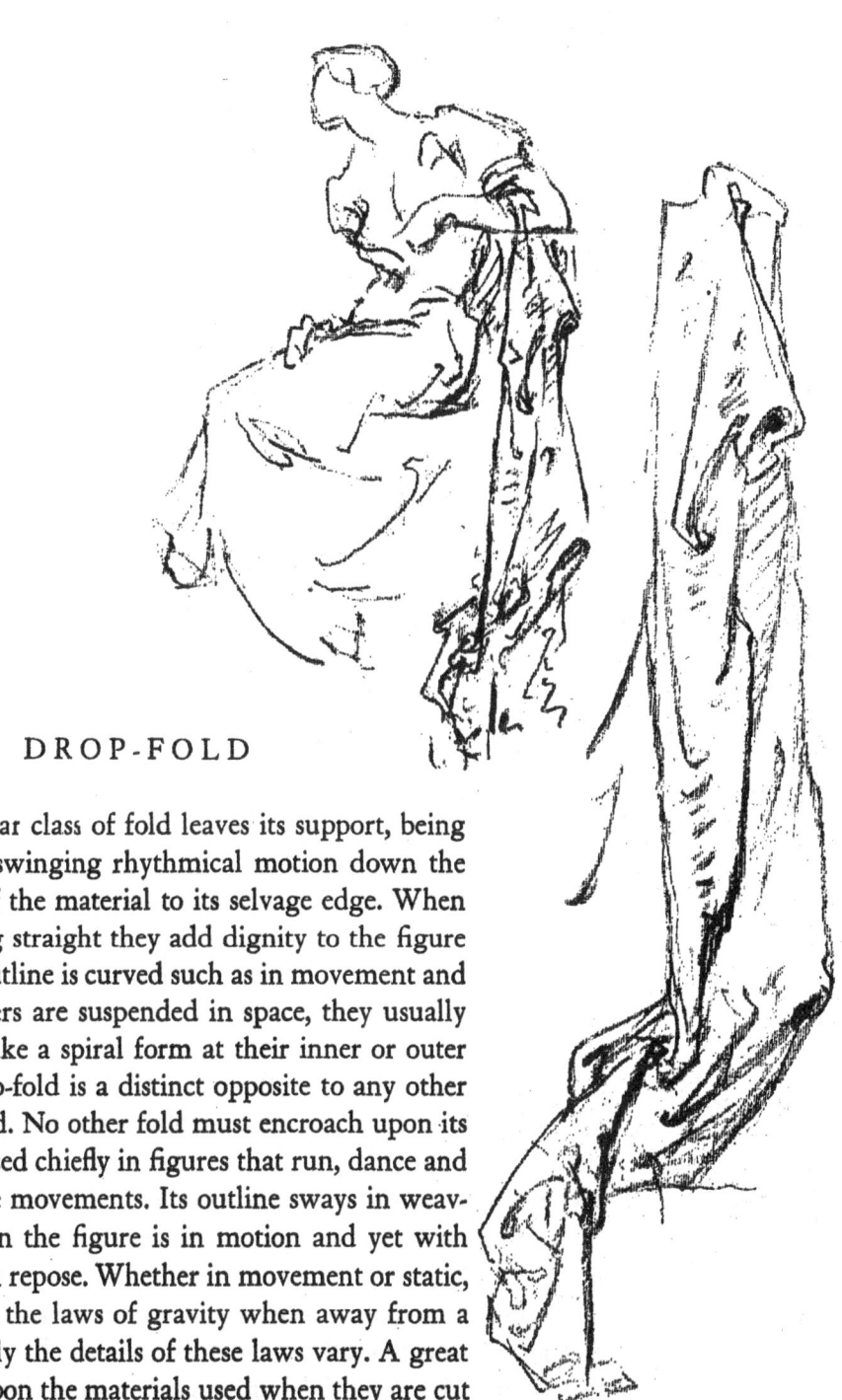

## DROP-FOLD

As THIS particular class of fold leaves its support, being
free, it takes a swinging rhythmical motion down the
whole length of the material to its selvage edge. When
these folds hang straight they add dignity to the figure
but when the outline is curved such as in movement and
the lower borders are suspended in space, they usually
twist, turn or take a spiral form at their inner or outer
edges. The drop-fold is a distinct opposite to any other
character of fold. No other fold must encroach upon its
territory. It is used chiefly in figures that run, dance and
other decorative movements. Its outline sways in weav-
ing curves when the figure is in motion and yet with
dignity when in repose. Whether in movement or static,
all folds follow the laws of gravity when away from a
fixed point. Only the details of these laws vary. A great
deal depends upon the materials used when they are cut
straight across or warp ways. They then behave differ-
ently in detail.

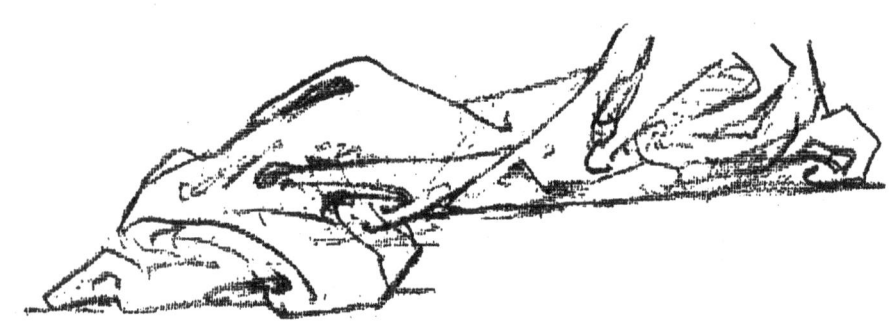

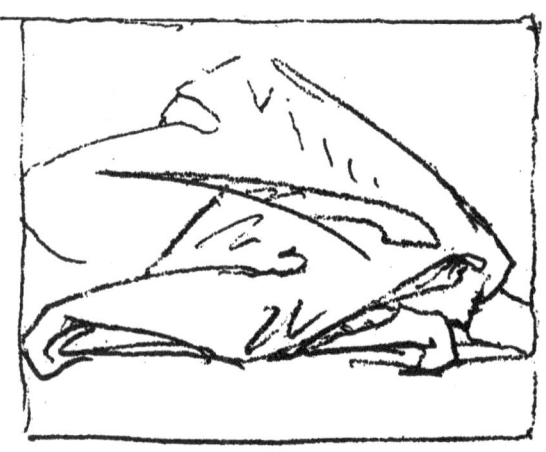

## INERT

IT IS understood, of course, that cloth no matter how thick or thin has in itself no given form. A piece of cloth when thrown or dropped on the floor either flattens out or crumples up and takes on a character distinct from any other form. This crumpled up piece of cloth is not static, it changes as it keeps settling, in an hour's time its vigorous angles become more subdued and flattened. Still it remains a fallen piece of goods with a character distinct and apart from any other, and this positive character must be the abstract idea back of the drawing to make it obvious to the onlooker that this fallen piece of cloth is inert and dead.

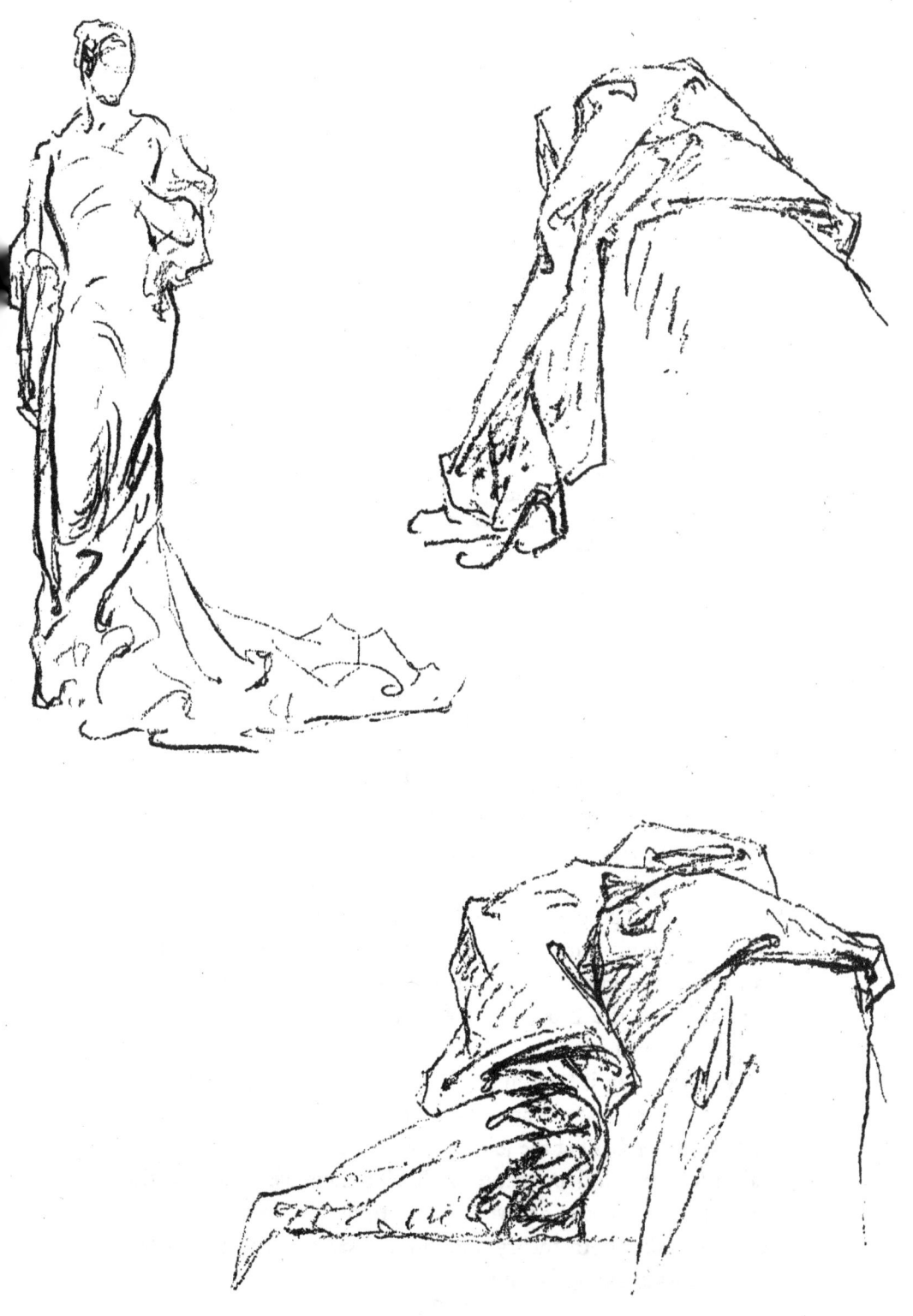

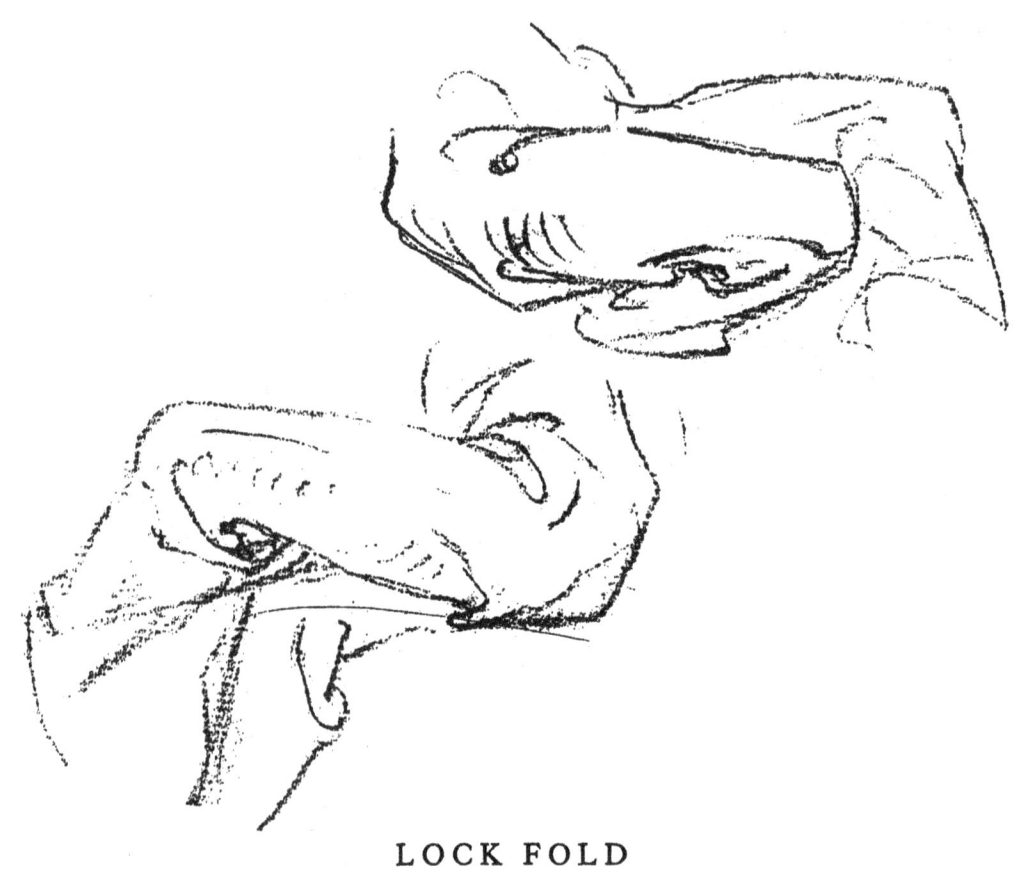

## LOCK FOLD

WHEN drawing folds that occur at the bending of a limb, it must be understood that drapery is either attached to, or supported at some fixed point. If the material is limited as to volume, such as the bending at the knee, the folds radiate in size and number from the fixed point of attachment as well as a point of resistance. The lower limbs vary greatly as to shape; below the hip the thigh is round, at the knee the form is square with its sides beveled forward and the broad double bellied calf muscle covers the upper half of the leg.

When the leg is bent upon the thigh at the knee, the two opposing masses that are above and below the knee need little detail, but when bent at the joint, the folds become bunched up and take on both spiral and acute angles. To memorize the direction and meaning of one or two of these folds gives a plan to work upon. It takes both theory and close observation to find a fold that occurs again and again.

[ 38 ]

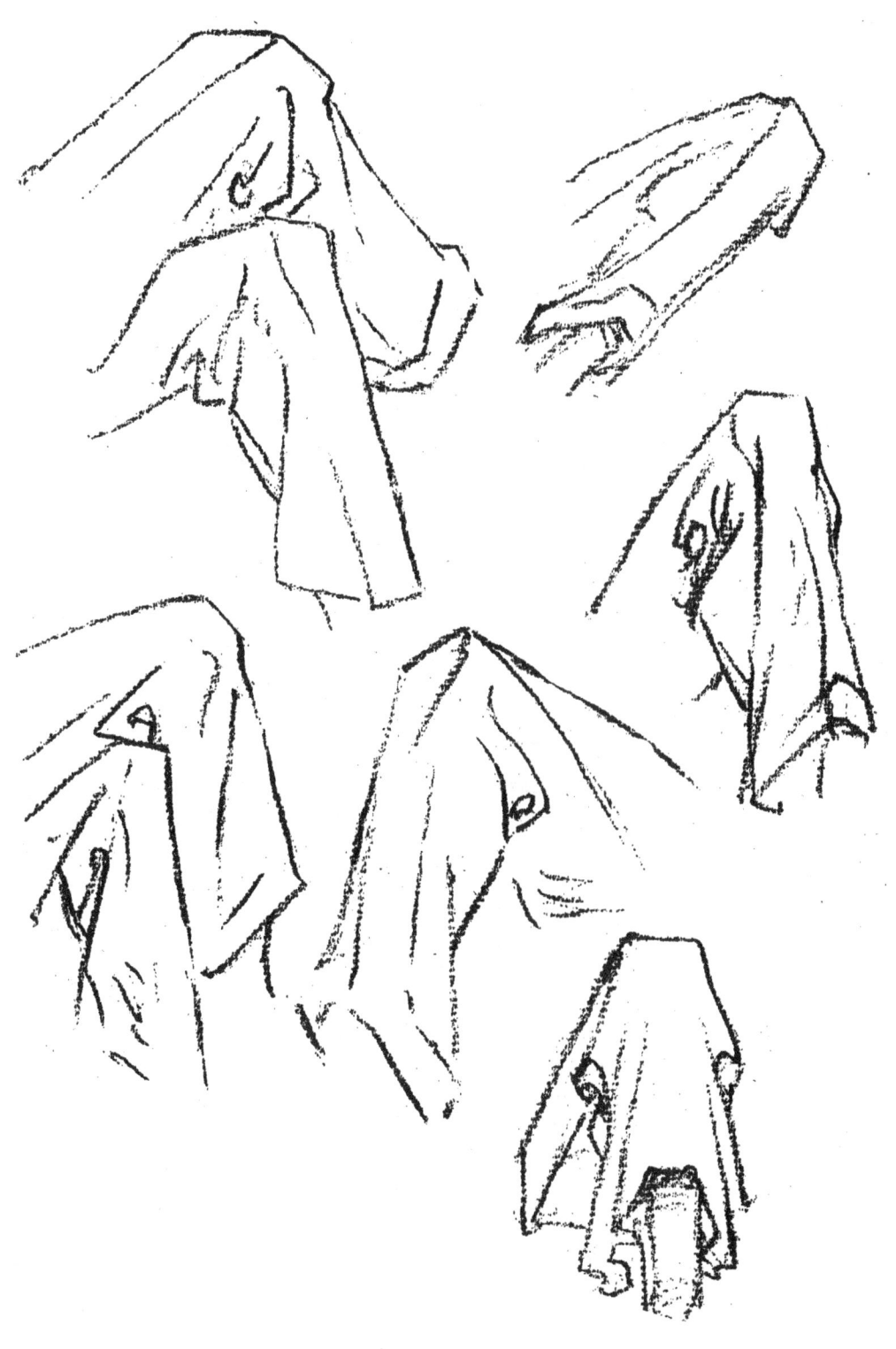

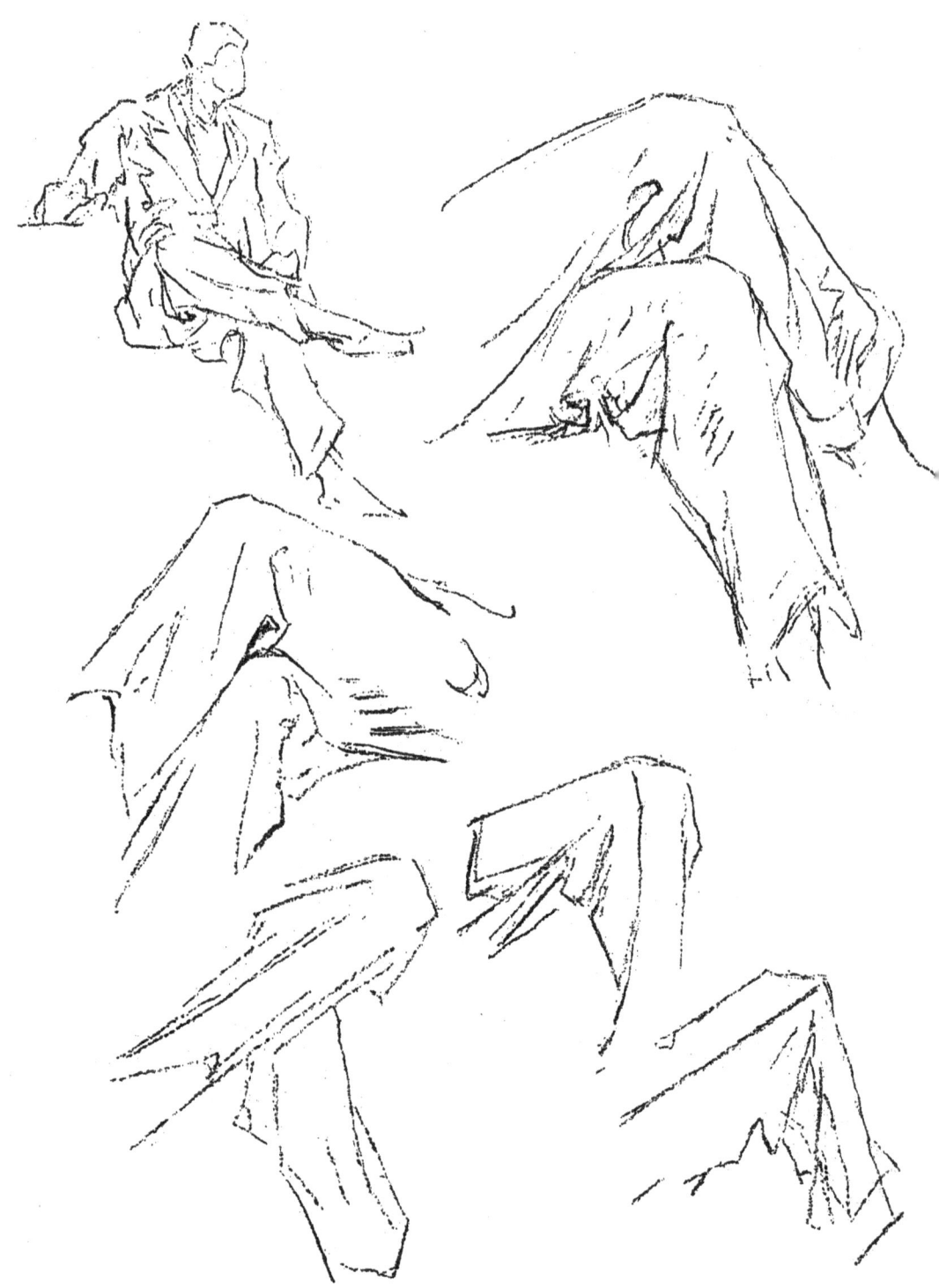

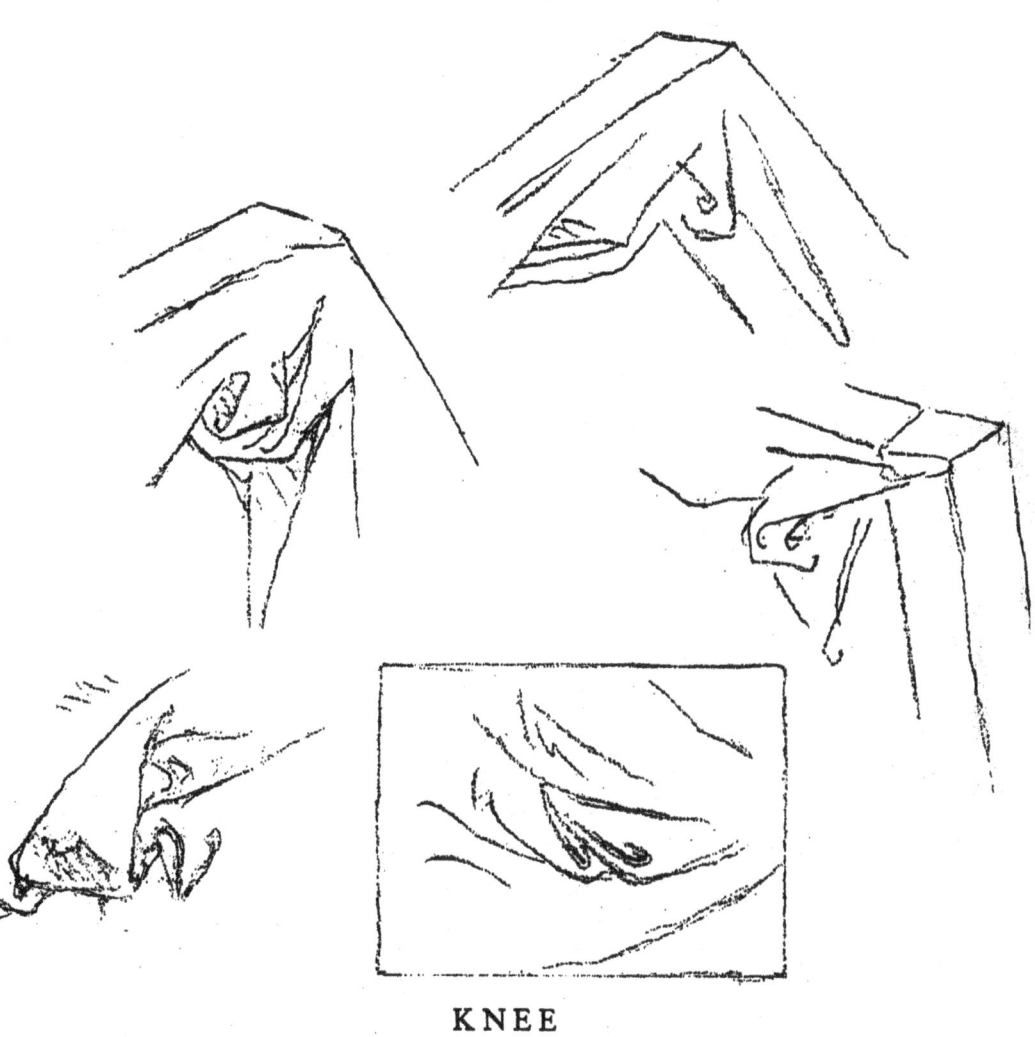

## KNEE

IN DRAWING folds look out for forms that happen and then happen again. Using this as a background, one can put in the really important things that are essential to the story and not just a series of still life studies describing things that are not worth describing. In studying the character of these different folds, the quality of materials should be tried out to study their comparative relationship, such as: the difference of weight and tension; heavier materials as compared to light or more pliant materials. Try to remember the folds that happen and then happen again and you will find a family resemblance in all materials no matter what the weight or texture.

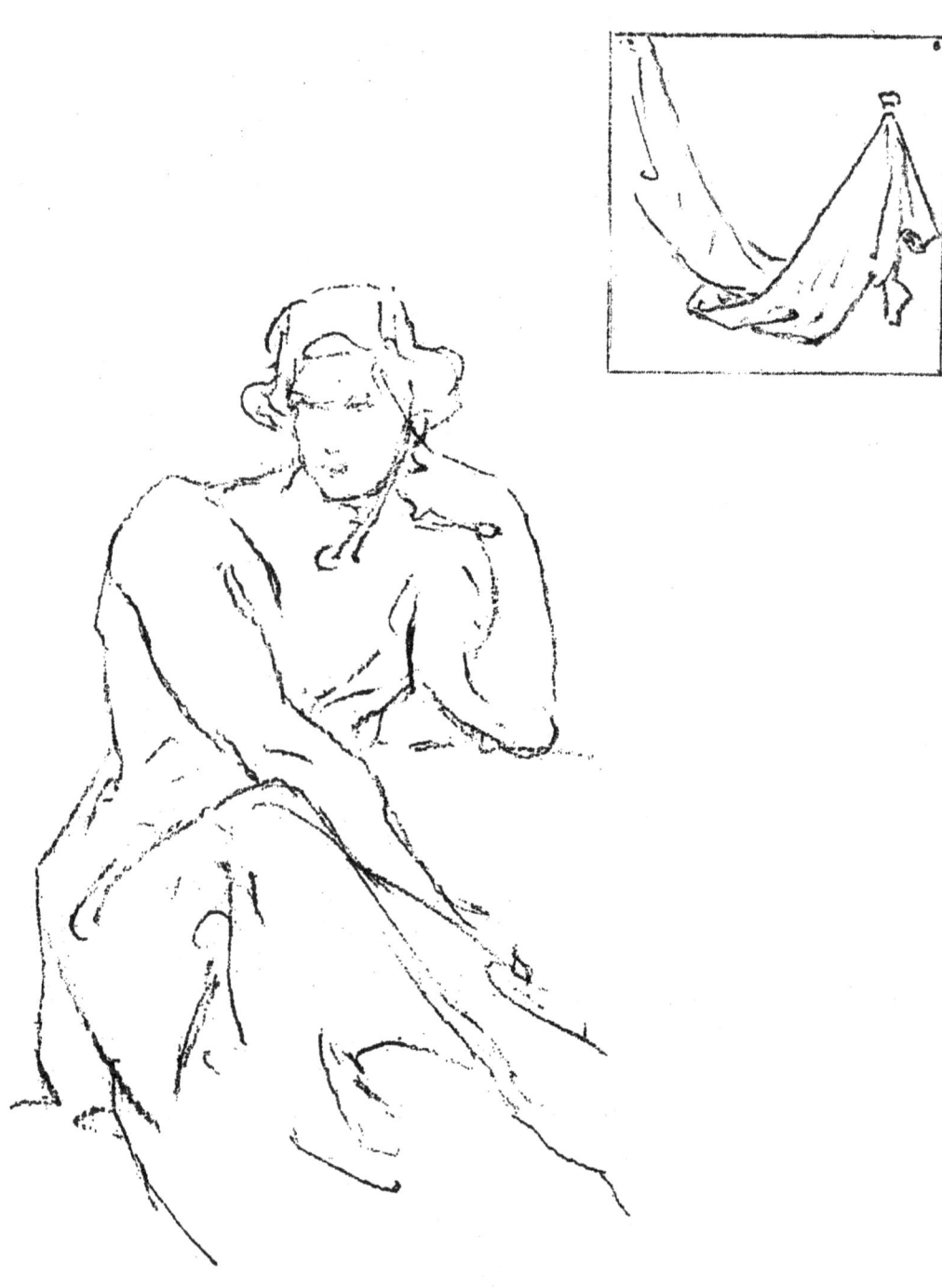

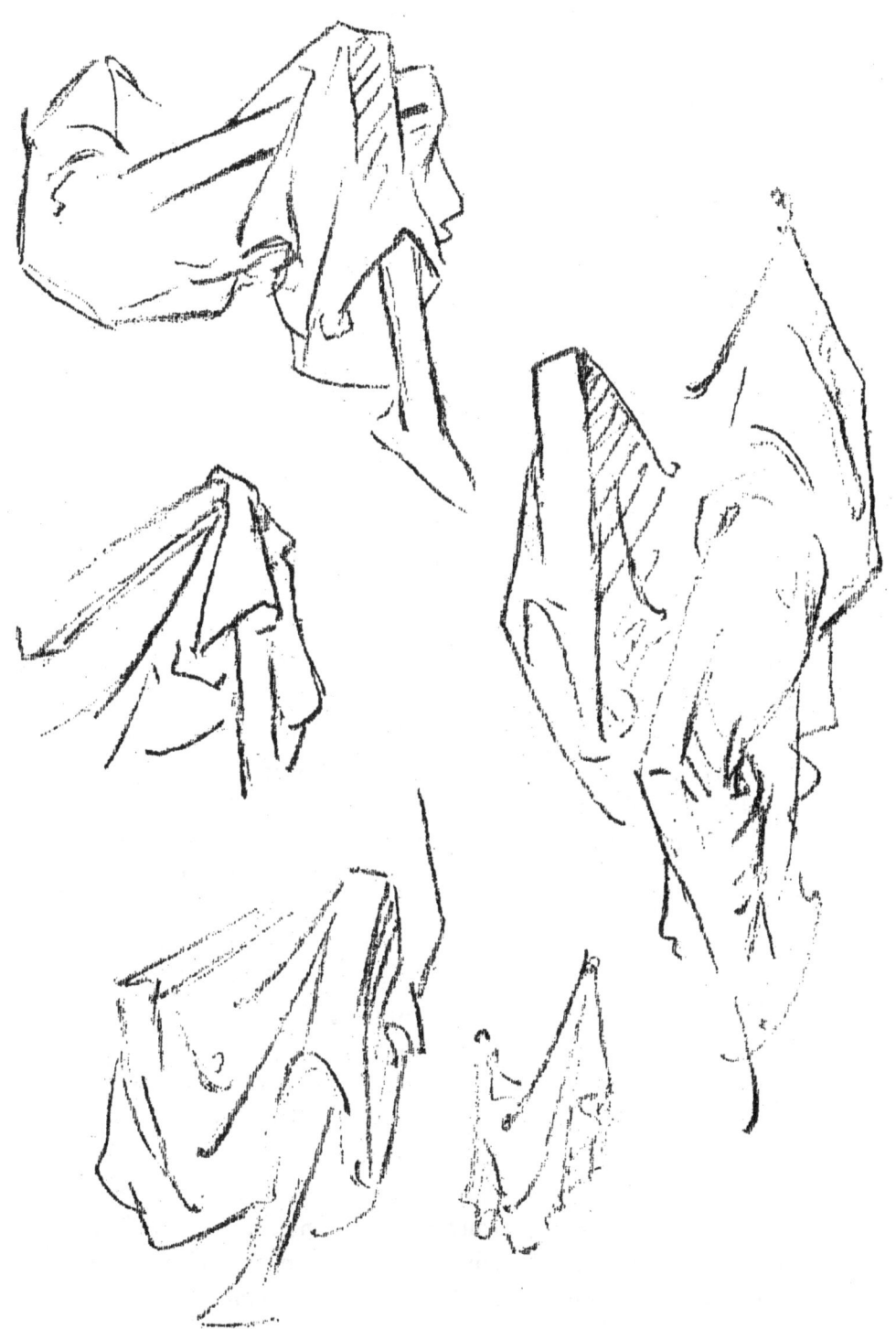

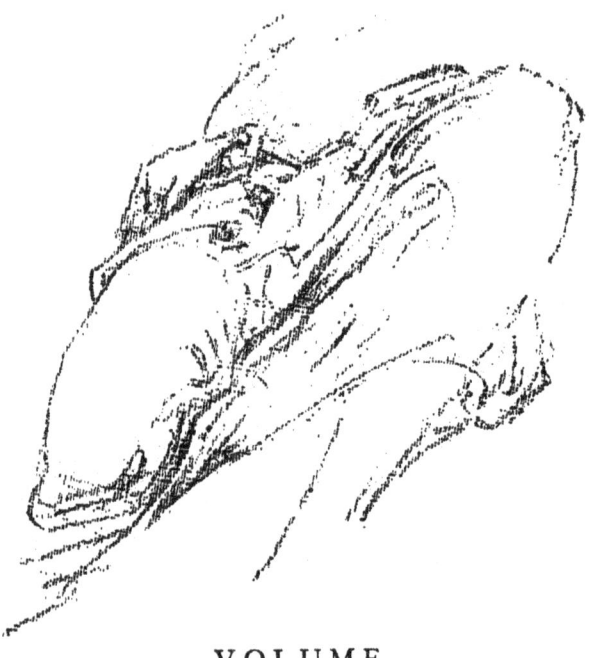

# VOLUME

THE treatment of heavy materials is more of a problem than that of lighter weight, for the reason that it is more difficult to preserve the real form of the body beneath and make it apparent that it represents a human figure and not just a mass of cloth and folds. Assuming that the principal supports of a sitting figure are from the knees, and that these supports are on a level horizontally and not too close together, the descending folds would festoon toward the center following the weight of the material causing the lower border to fan out and become more pointed below and lower down than at the sides. Should one foot be resting on a stool or cushion then one support would be higher than the other causing a large festoon above and a smaller one below to interlock much nearer the lower knee than at the center. In this case the folds would not be continuous from one support to the other but would meet at a more acute angle.

When drapery hangs in loose folds the opposing festoon and cones do not interlock at acute angles but intermingle and fade into each other. The thought must be to carry the idea that a fold is doing a definite thing. It is your understanding as well as copying that makes the drawing of drapery possible.

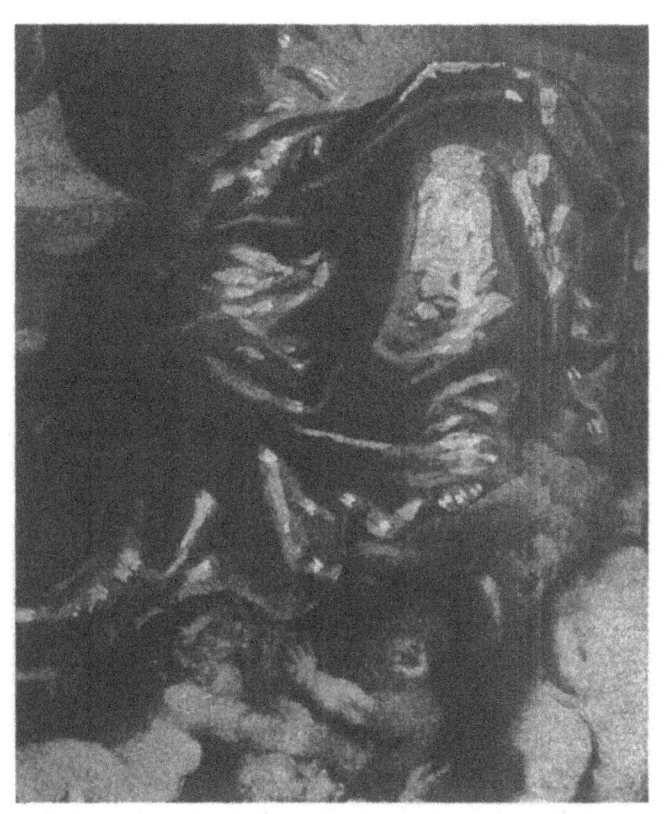

RUBENS

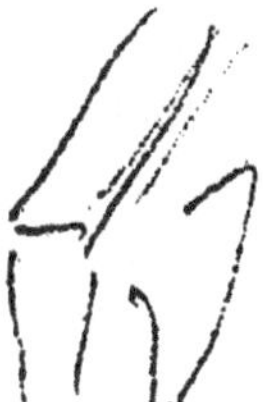

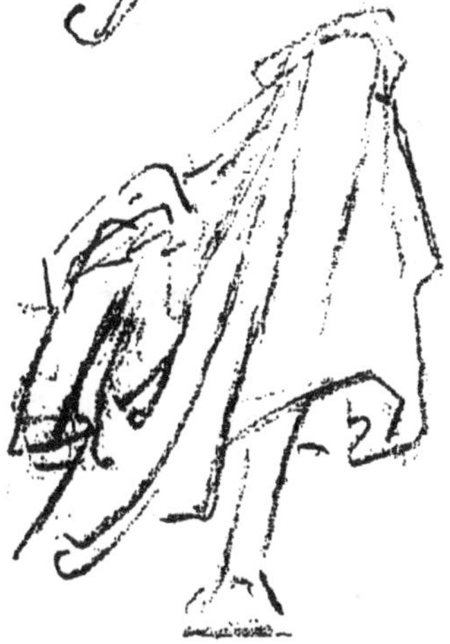

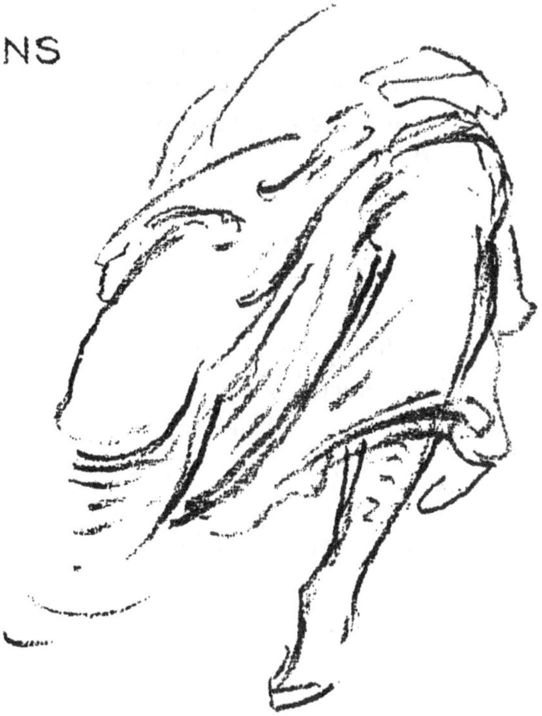

FOLDS must be arranged and regulated to the lines of the figure. Folds that fall some distance from the source of support shake or wave irregularly as they leave the figure. These may be seen as concave or convex according to the way it is connected to the cordage of the material. The upper portion may have the same width or bulk, but having less space it gives a pipe-like appearance above. As it descends it widens out and becomes more free at the lower borders. These descending folds must have the appearance of falling from their support above, such as the shoulder, sleeve or girdle. In drawing a drop or flying fold one must sense and force it to drop, no camera can give these qualities, they are personal, individual. A photograph may be useful in studying the details of parts, but could scarcely be of use in the arrangement of, we will say, two figures or more. A camera may be as accurate as the human eye, but it cannot render the beauty of line or the arrangement that enters into the expression demanded by the many factors that go to make a composition. A photograph does not eliminate the petty details that go to make folds convincing. The different characters of folds that are represented here must not be looked on as a novelty. Drapery that falls free of the figure must give the impression of descending or flying, the idea must be to carry this impression to others, that this piece of drapery is doing a definite thing. It is your understanding of these simple laws that will make the drawing of drapery possible and convincing.

To get an idea of drapery in motion, have someone express the movement you have in mind by swinging a length or so of thin or heavy material in a backward, a forward or a rhythmical movement. At the same time, hold a piece of tissue paper in one hand and twist or turn it with the other hand until it is given somewhat the duplicate motion you wish, then thumb-tack the tissue to a board and copy the details. For heavier goods, a heavier piece of paper should be used.

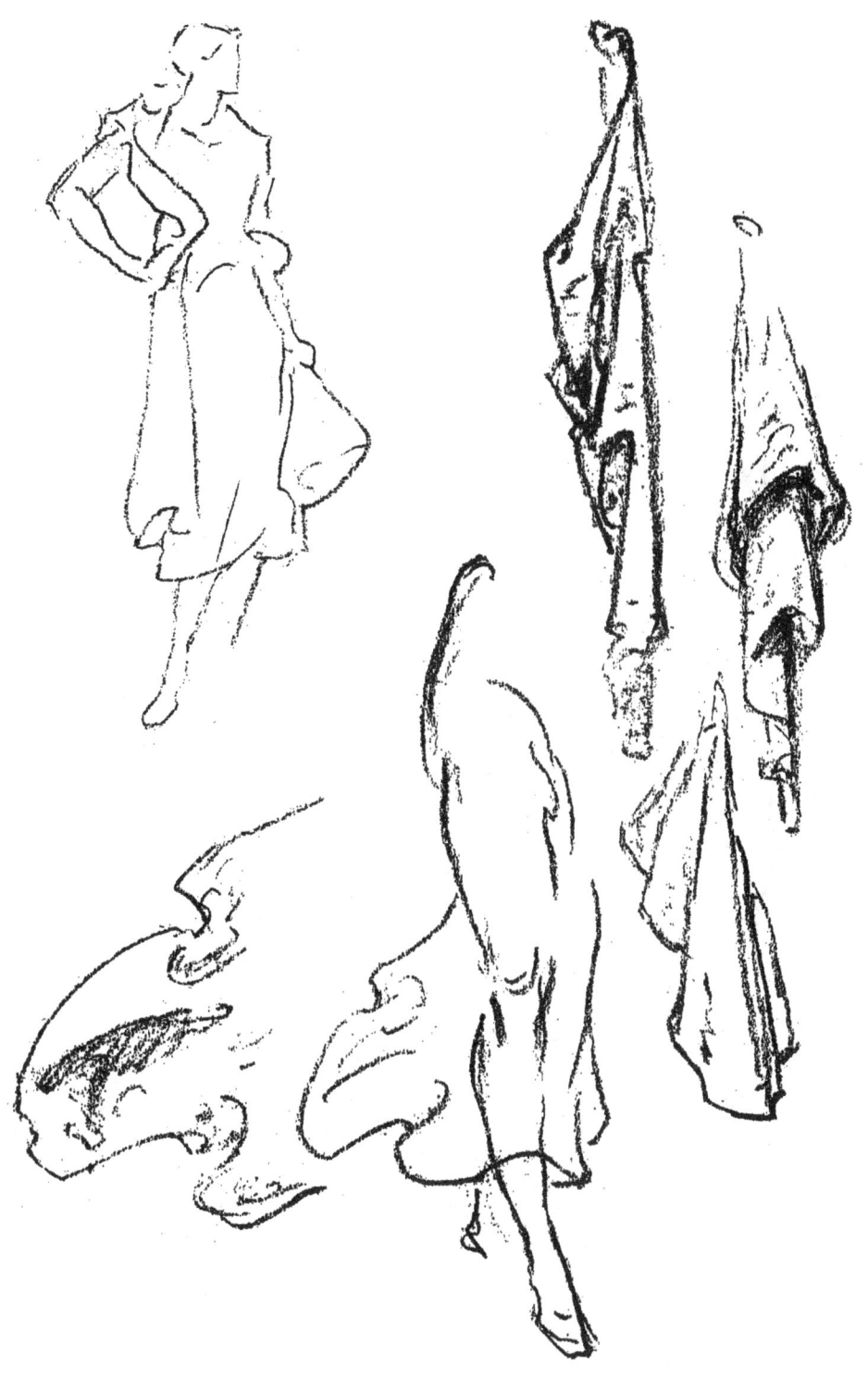

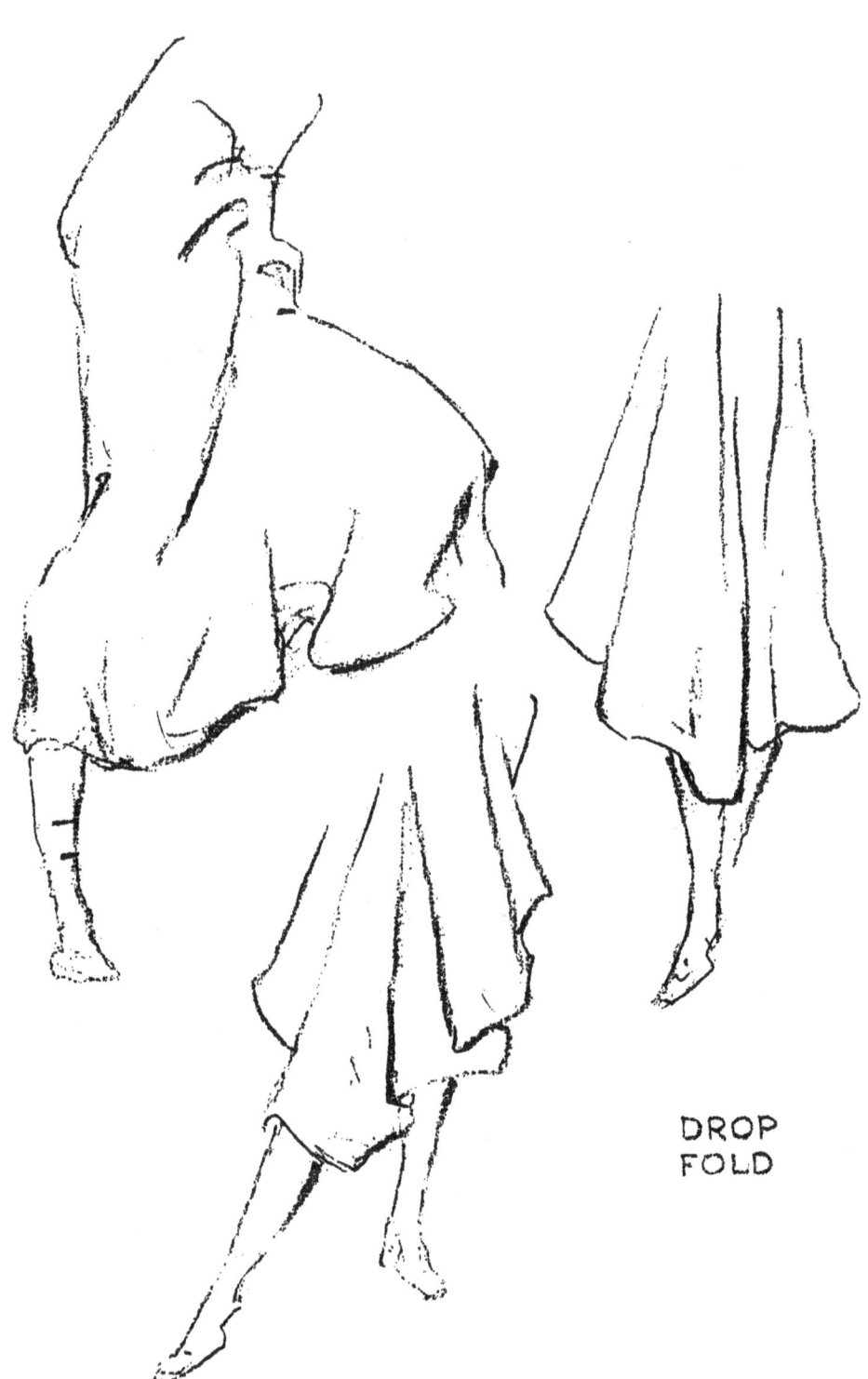

DROP
FOLD

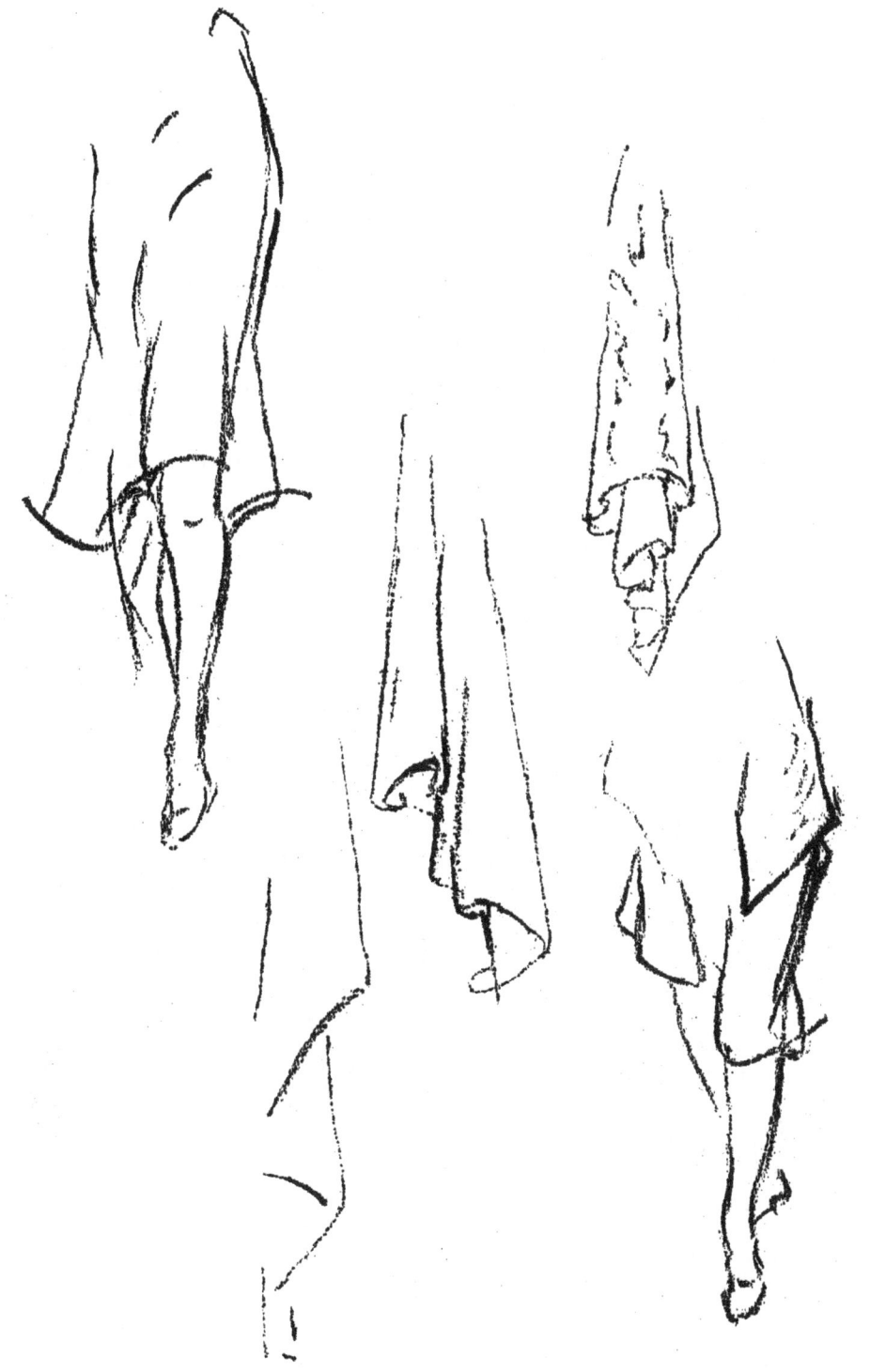

DRAPERY when attached to the shoulder or girdle falls downward and radiates from the points of support. If they meet as they descend they fan out and usually dissolve into one graceful fold but when the material has two or more points of support, they usually meet as angles or zigzags at their points of intersection. Once these facts are understood by the student, folds have a meaning, while to the casual observer all folds look alike.

All materials whether thick or thin follow the laws of gravity. It must be understood also, that it is the variation of these common laws that give character and charm to a drawing. Again, every line and every form of fold is dominated by the construction of the body beneath.

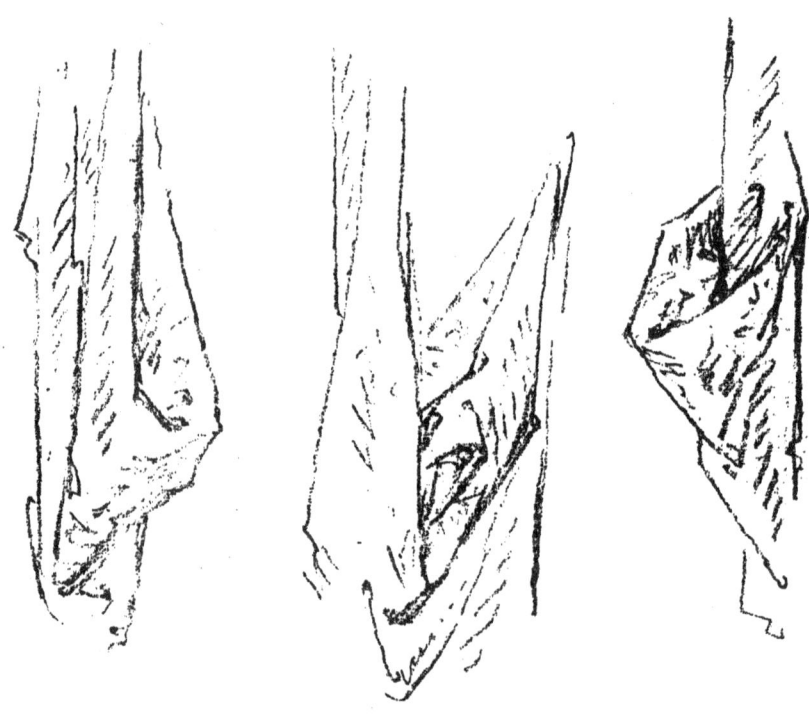

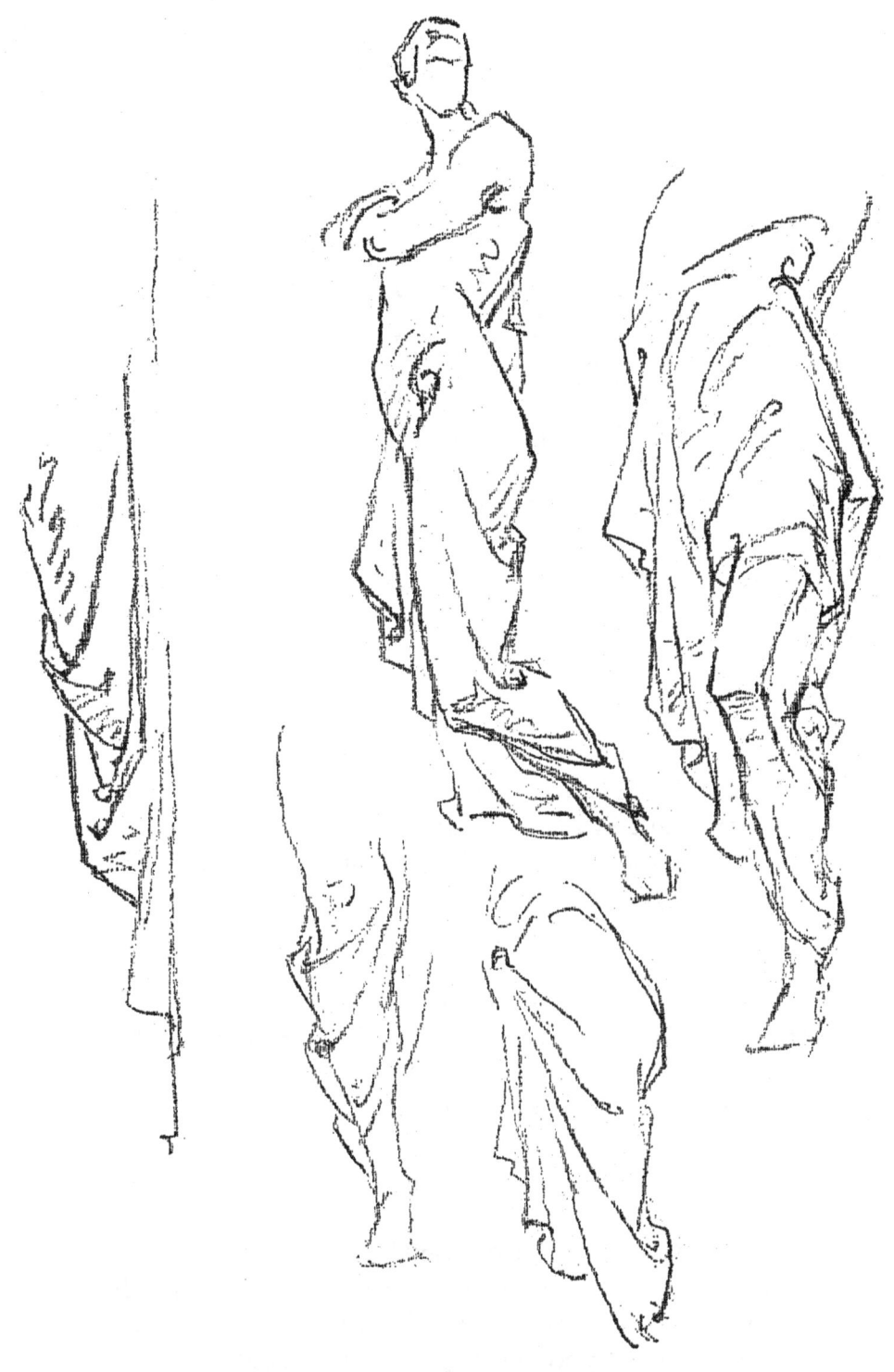

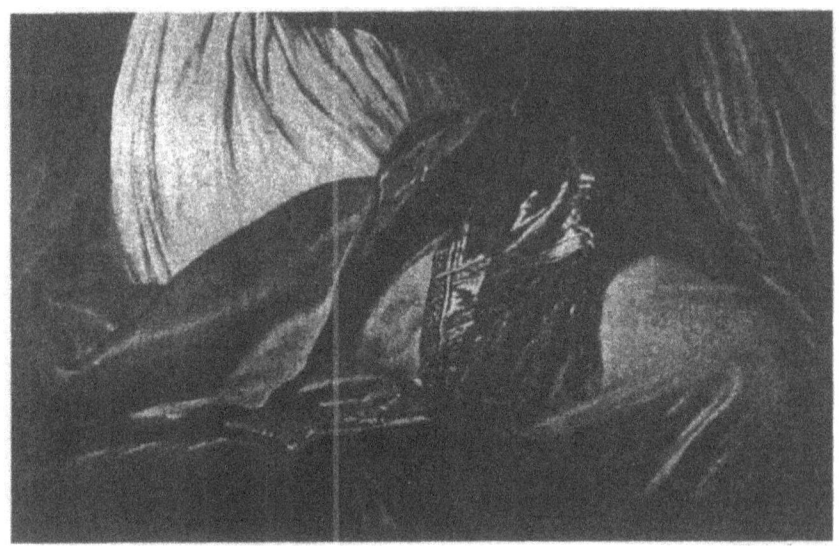

## ARRANGEMENT OF FOLDS

THOUGH one can copy a piece of drapery by noting every fold or crease, it will be observed that every time the model moves, the folds seem to take on a different aspect. Therefore, some underlying principle must be thought out or there will be little harmony as a whole.

Cloth revolves itself into drapery but the thought that must be carried out is the idea of a figure draped with a body underneath. This fact must always be uppermost. Next, the art is in the arrangement which comprises line, rhythm, distribution and subordination, grouping and balance, and the joining of all these essentials into a harmonious whole.

The character of drapery has followed the different periods in art as well as distinguishing the work of some particular master. Therefore, it must be realized that the object could not have been a servile imitation of folds. These periods varied from V shaped kinks at one time to long rounded festoons at another. The costumes of classic times were more suited to the study of the laws of folds than at the present time. The Greek paintings on pottery kept to long, flowing or sweeping lines that terminated in hook-like forms; the Gothic changed from round to angular; the Renaissance period shows a radiation of line that follows the figure allowing the plain surfaces to cling or lie close to the form thereby accentuating the figure beneath.

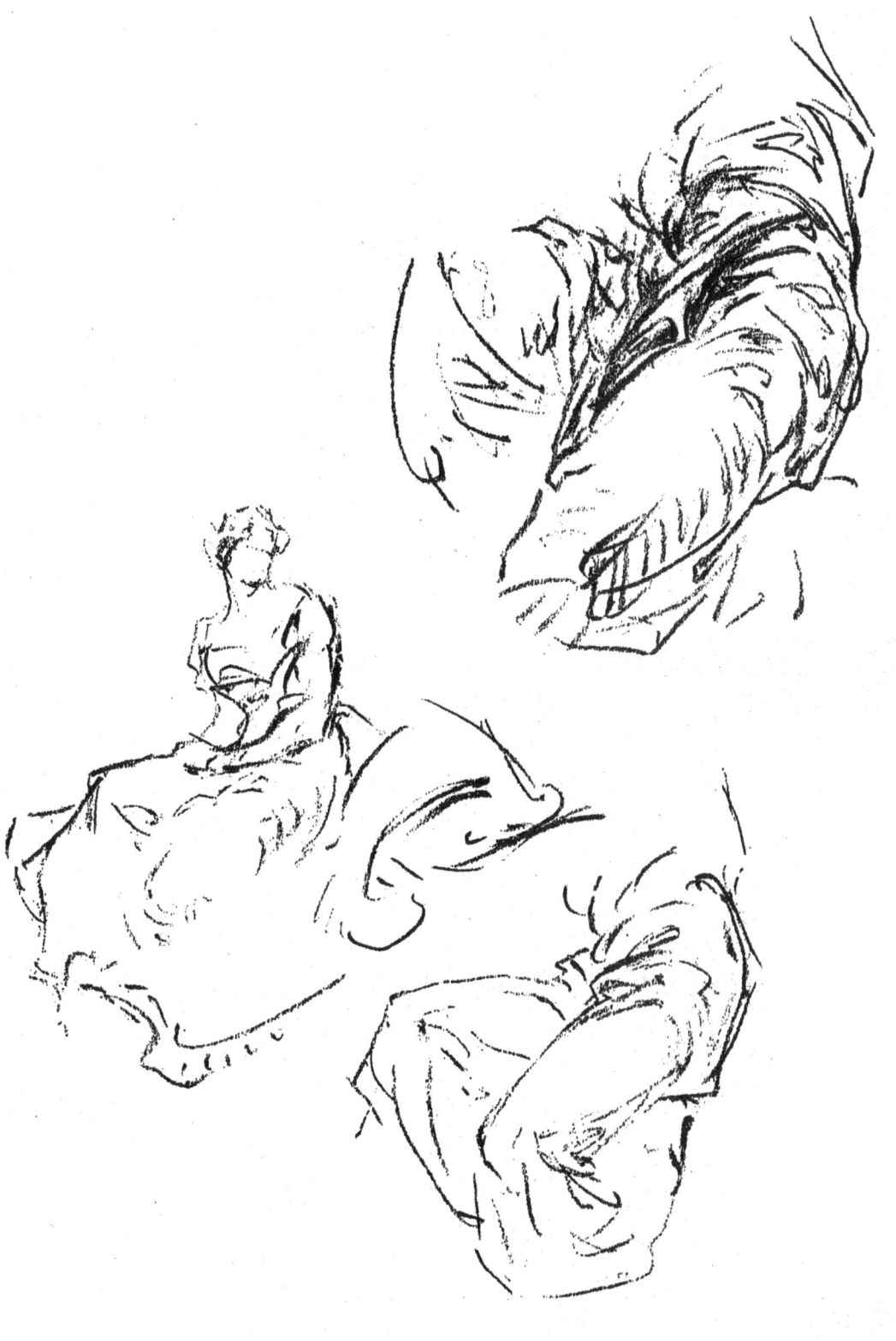

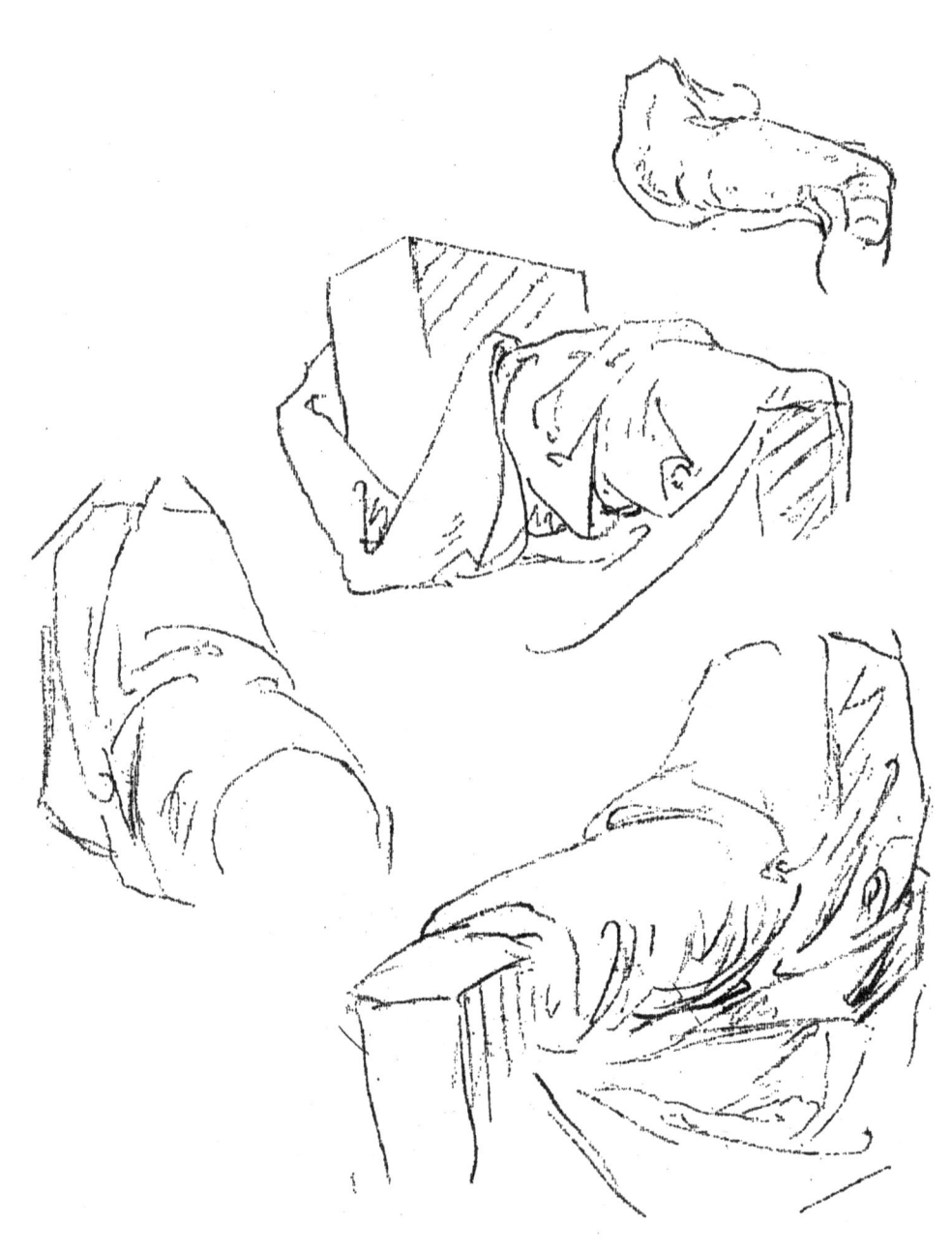

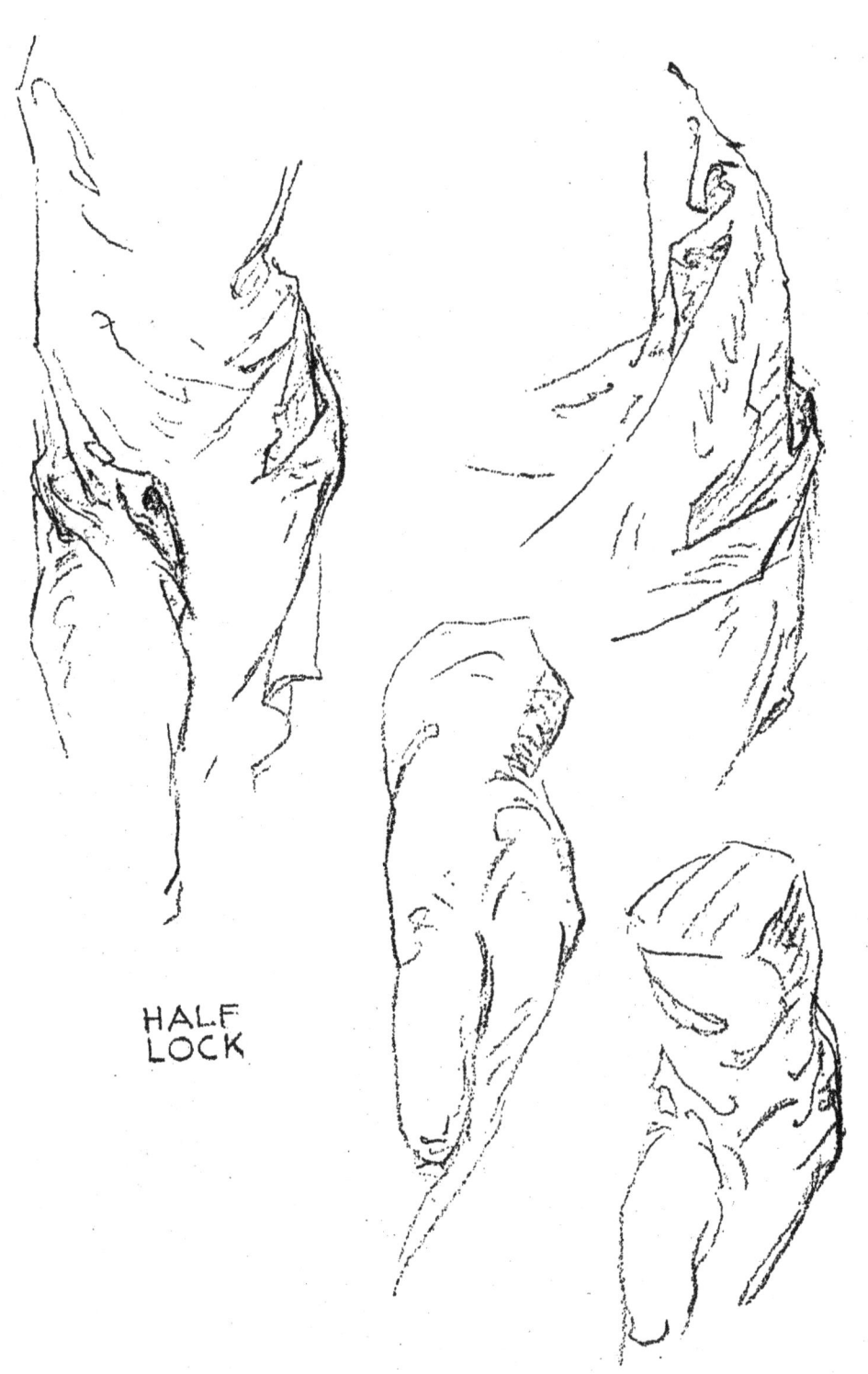

HALF
LOCK

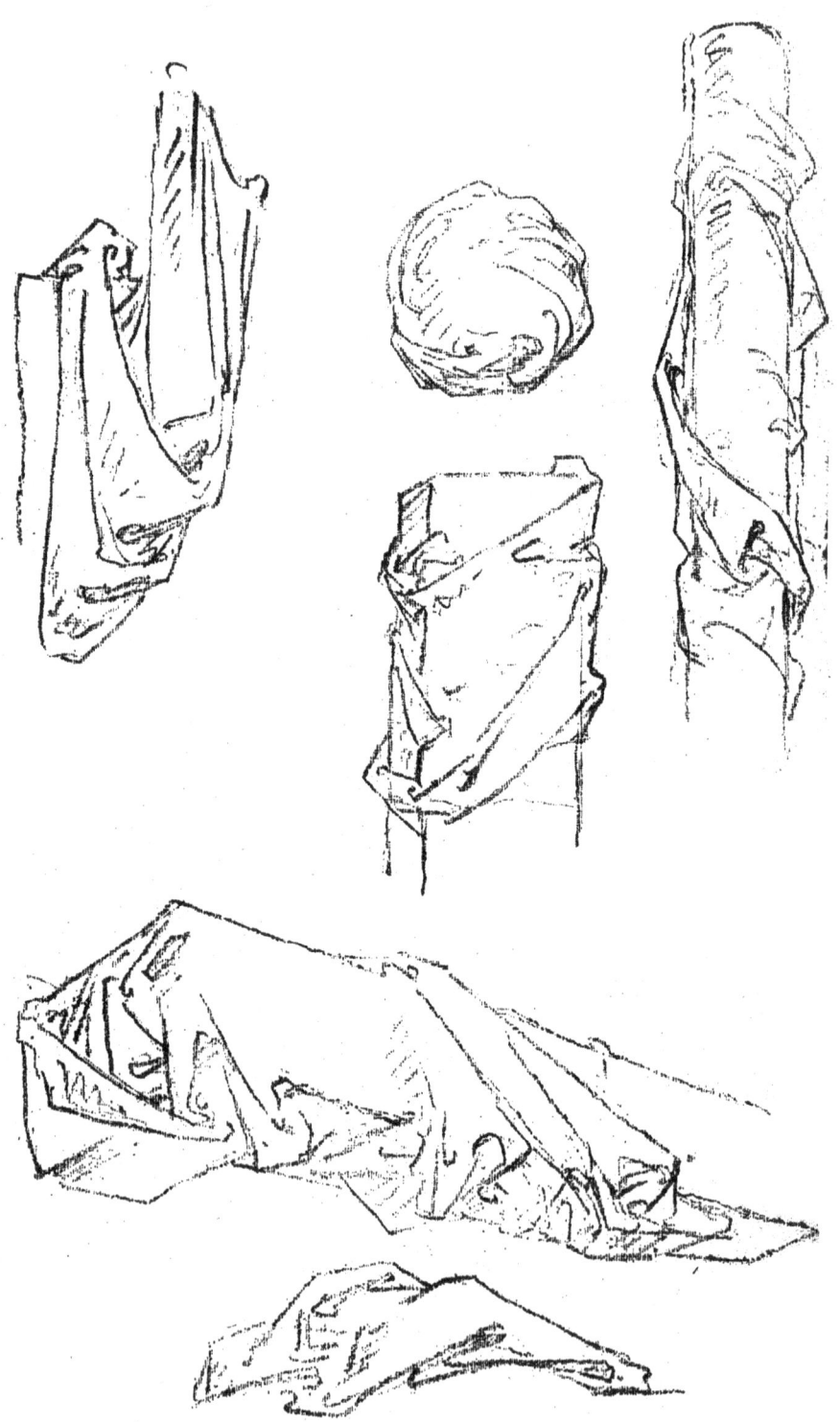

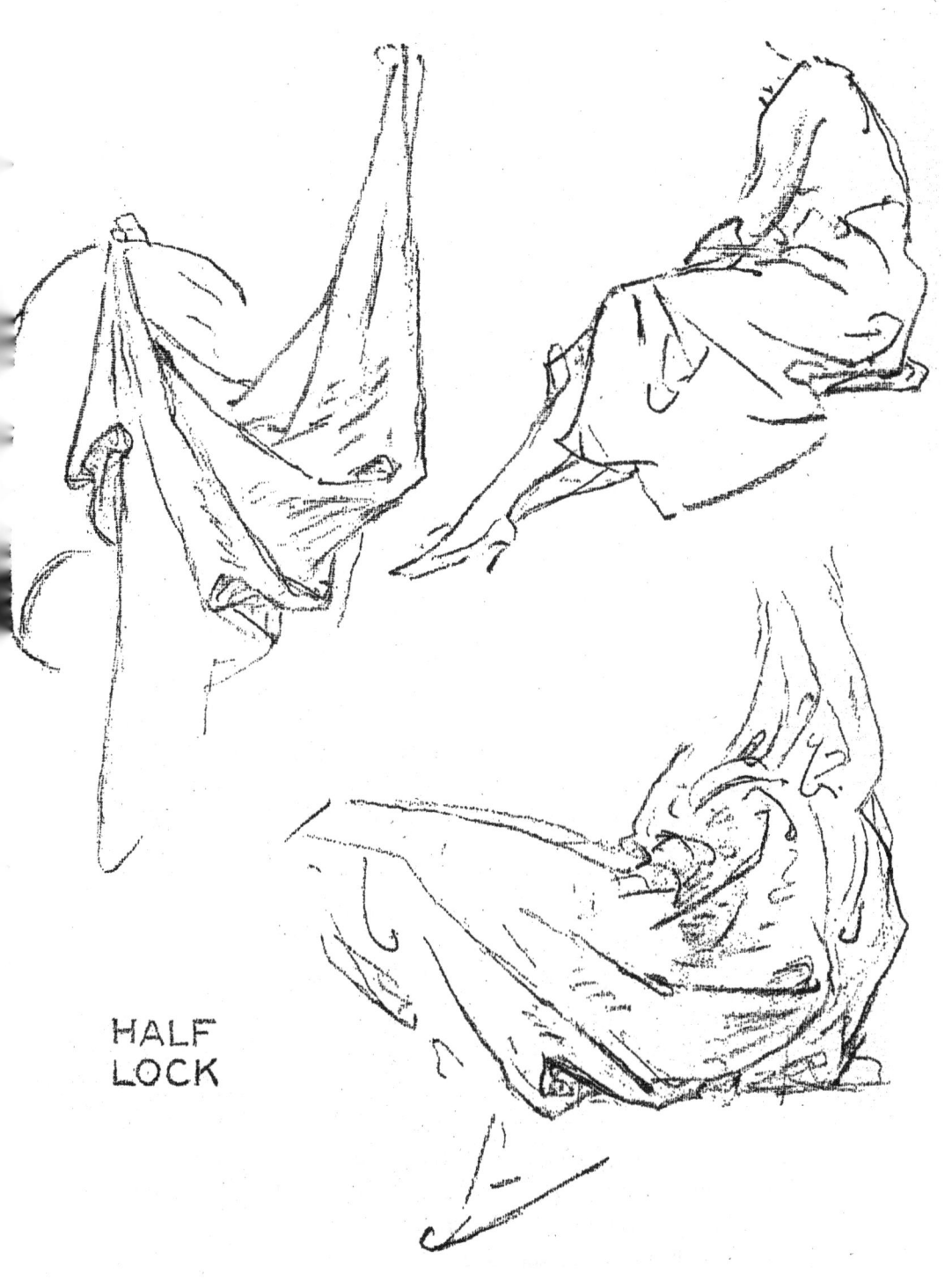

HALF
LOCK

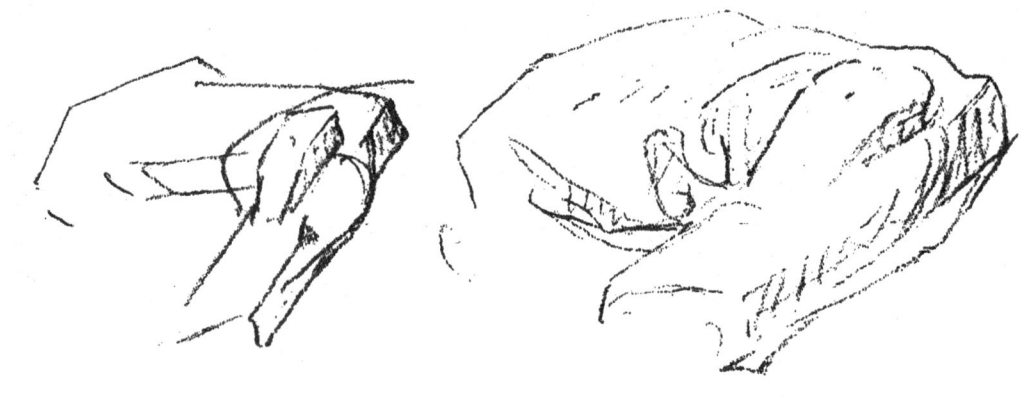

## ARM AND FOREARM

FABRICS follow the varied shapes of the body. They change in character every time a different direction of the body or limb occurs. When considering a sleeved or draped arm, the masses that lie underneath must be considered. The masses of the arm and forearm are joined by wedges and wedging movements that overlap each other at various angles. The shoulder slopes down and out, its broad side facing outward, the upper arm flattened at the sides. The mass of the forearm overlaps the end of the arm on the outside by a wedge that arises a third of the way up and tapers toward the wrist. Whether the arm is straight or bent, this wedge, this underlying form must be kept in mind. The folds pass over and around it; the creases alternating between round, zigzag or locked yet seldom paralleling one another.

The mass of the upper half of the forearm is oval in shape when the thumb is turned away from the body and more round when the thumb side of the hand is reversed. The forearm as it approaches the wrist becomes flattened out to about twice as wide as it is thick. As material has no form in itself, these round and wedged forms must be shown or felt under the material that covers the arm. The folds at the elbow under certain conditions can be looked upon and copied as a piece of still life, but if the points of attachments and resistance, as well as their radiating lines are understood, the translation of the form beneath is clearer and better understood.

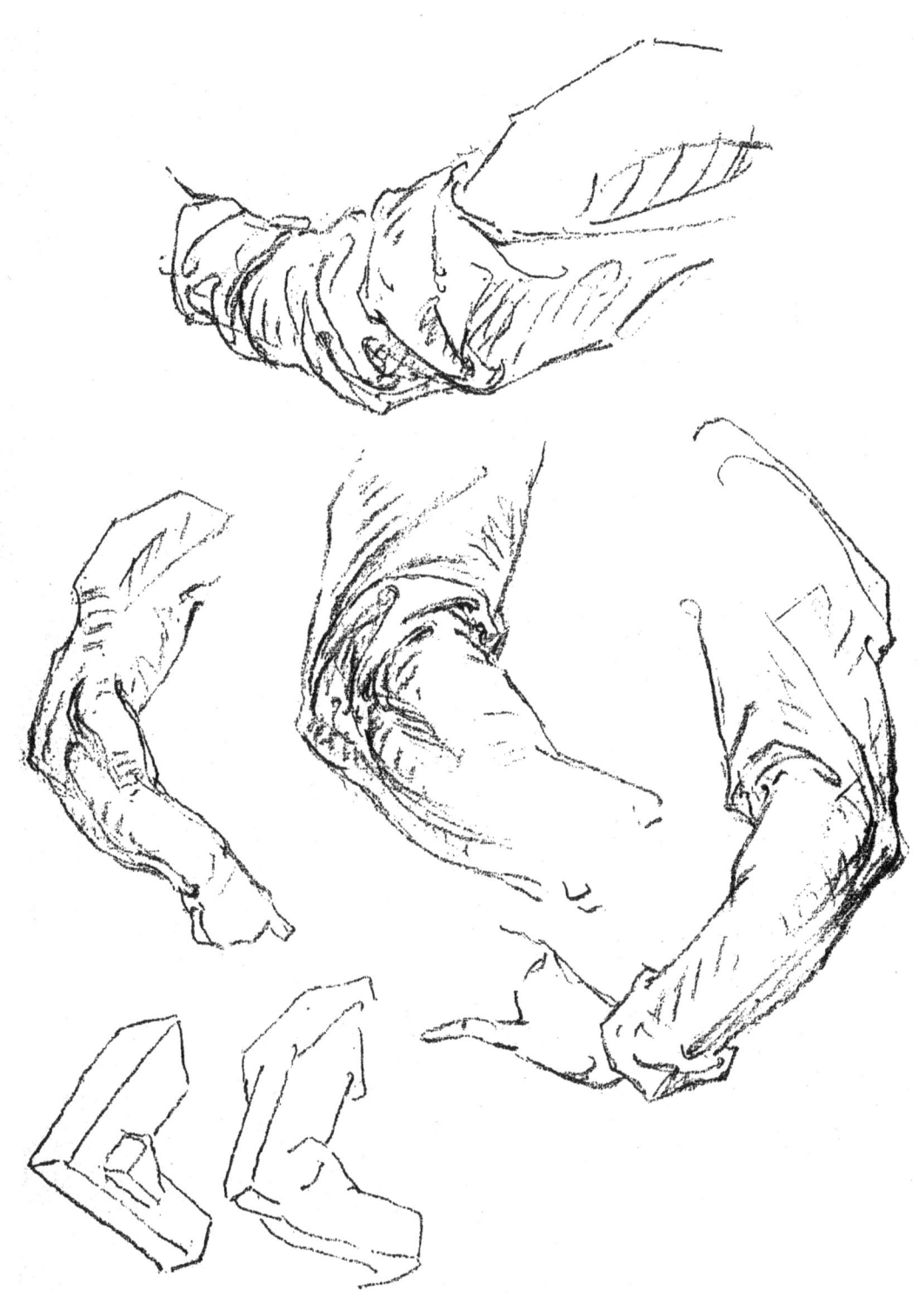

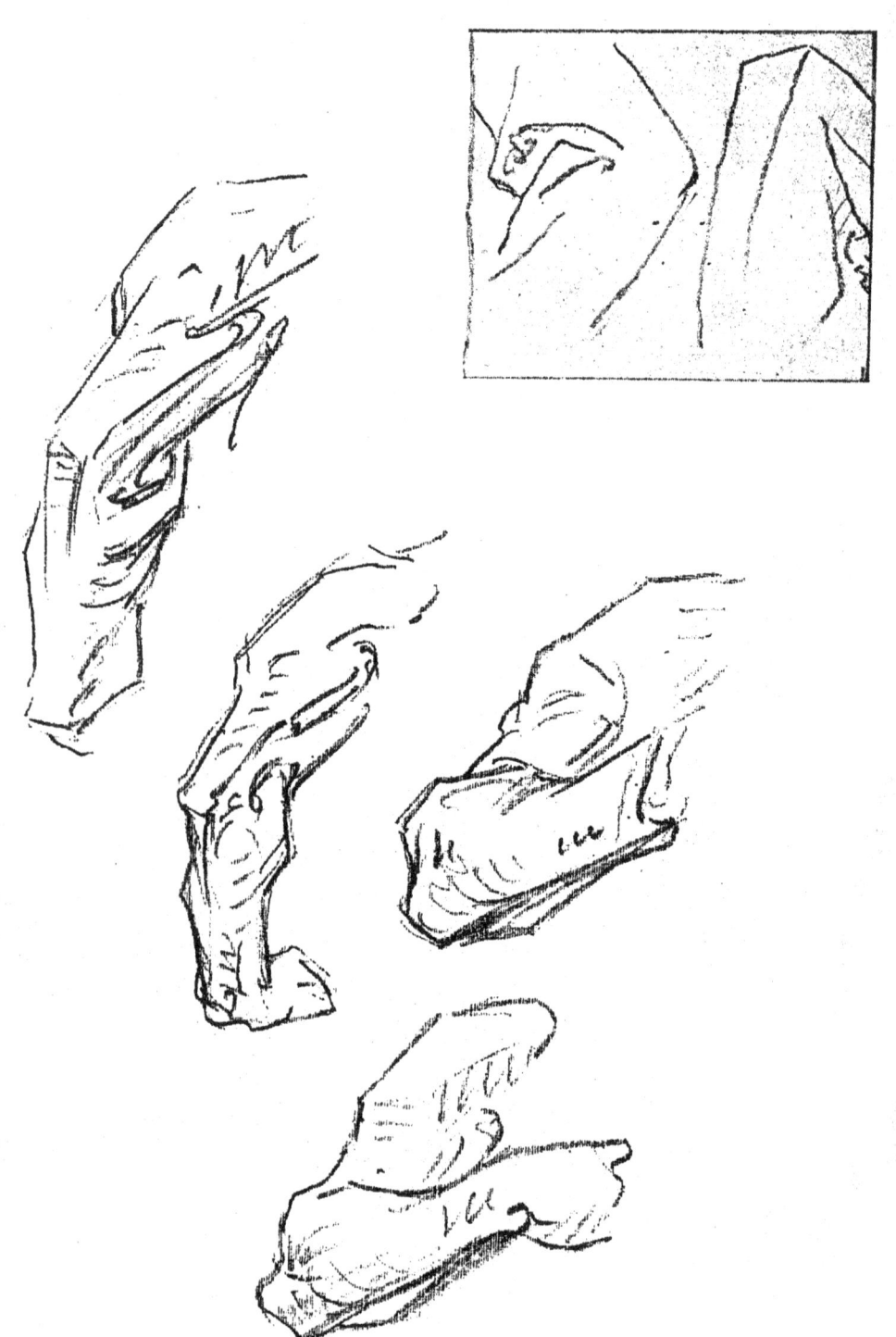

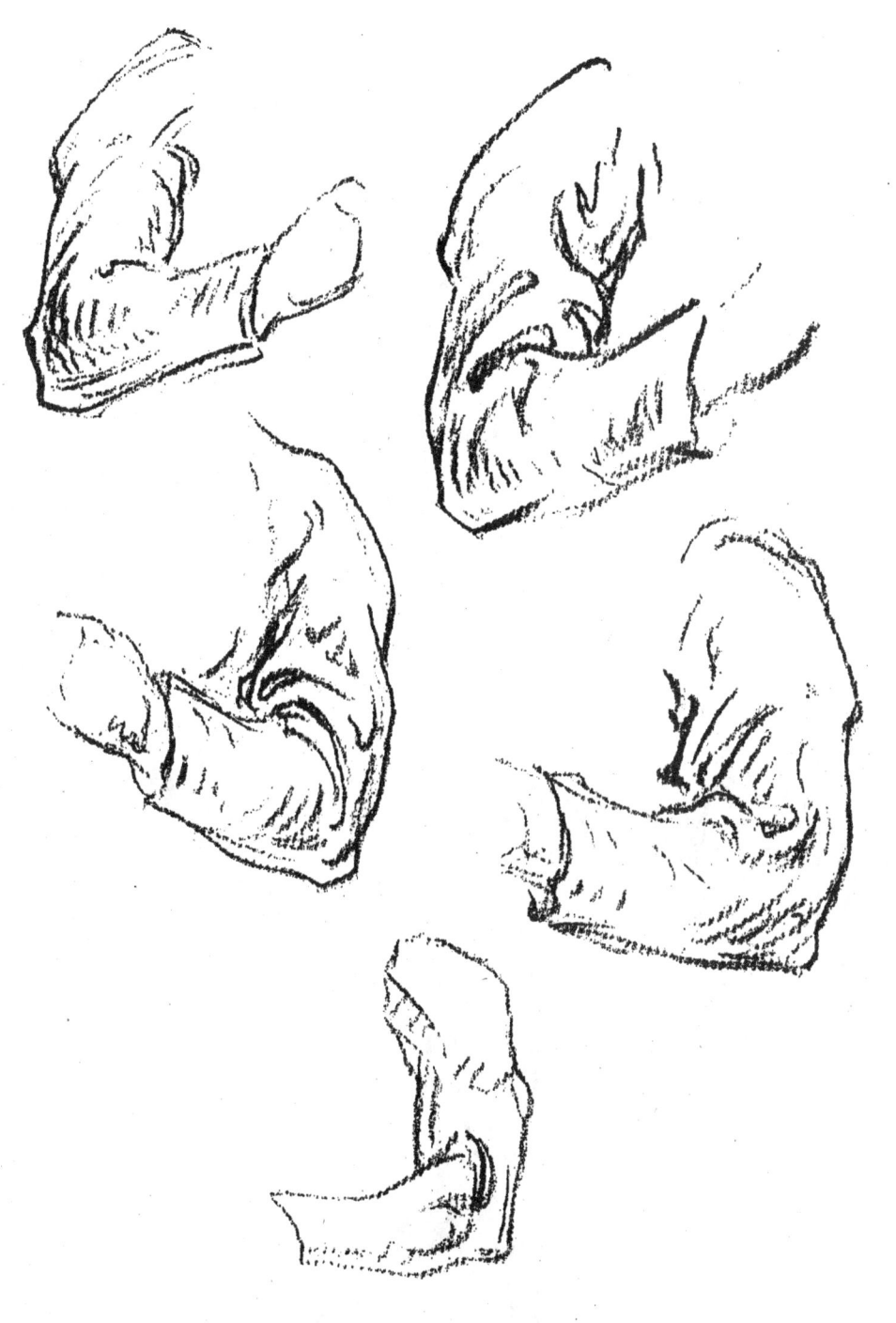

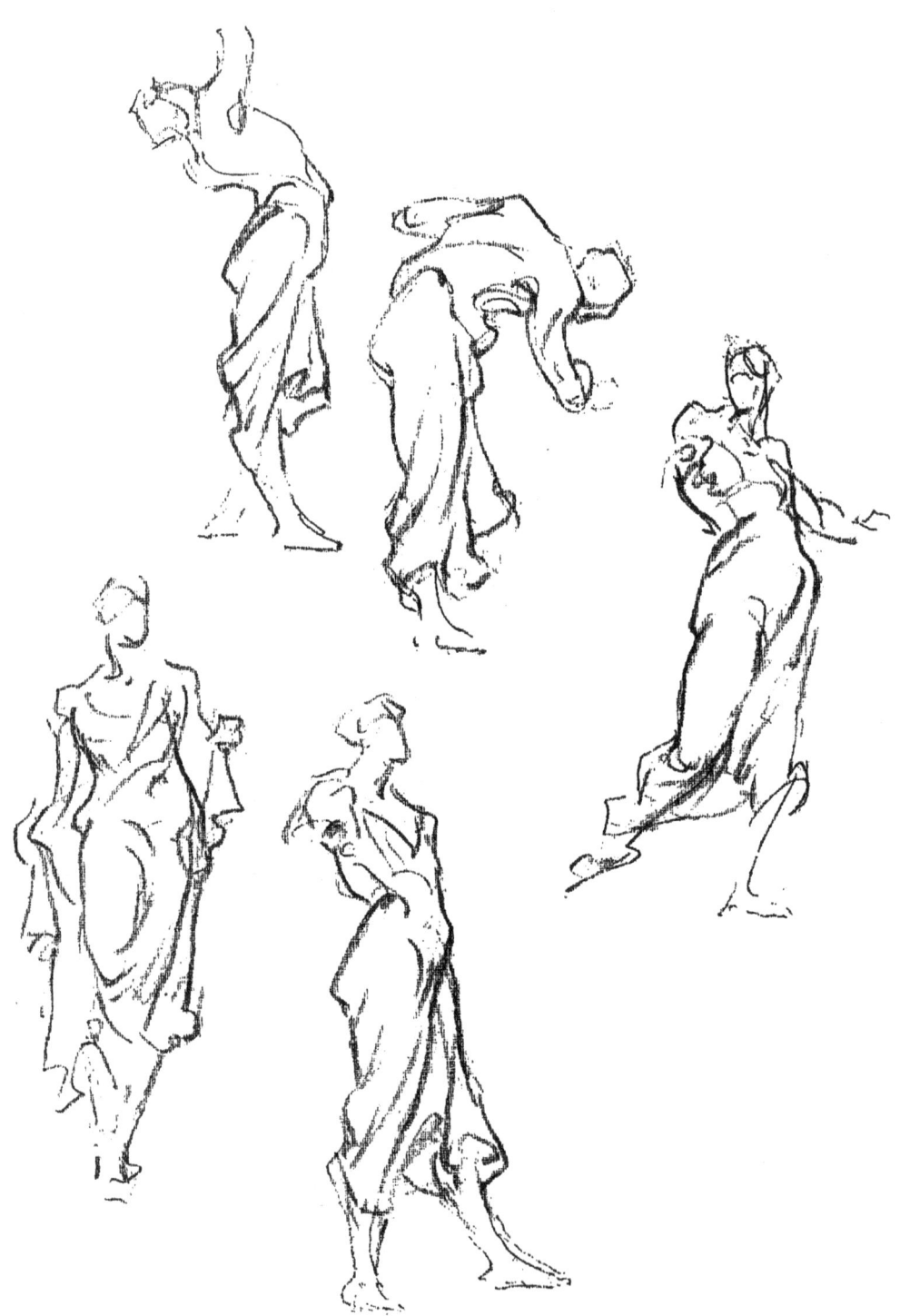

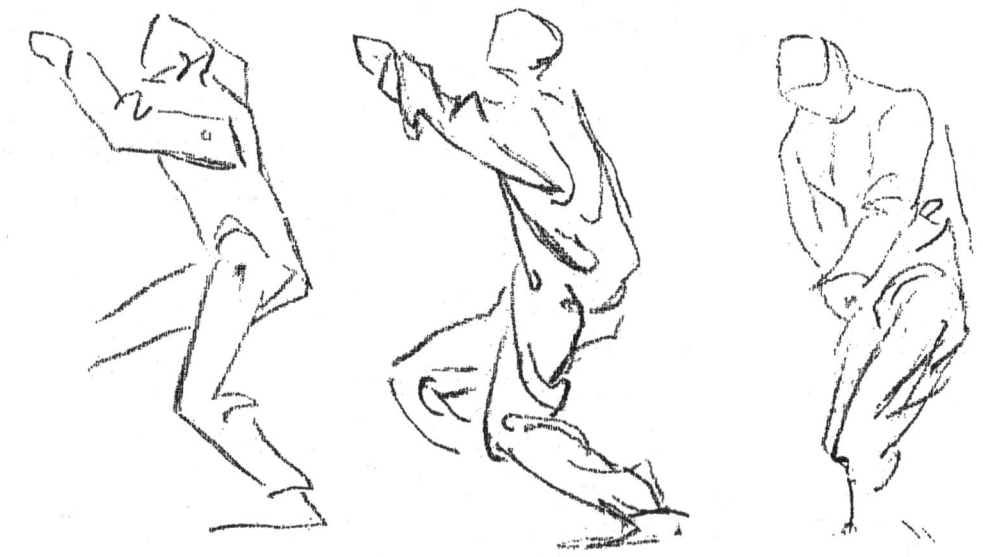

## DRAPED FIGURE

IT IS understood of course, that a figure must first be outlined, drawn or suggested before it can be properly clothed. Clothes are supported from the shoulder, the waist-band and at the hips in the costumes of both men and women. The principles of suspension are the same. Clothes are made loose enough so that the body can have great freedom of action, allowing the limbs to move freely in every possible way. These different actions in drapery are represented by lines radiating from the points of support terminating in hooks or hanging festoon-like from opposite systems. In case the folds are drawn upward in place of being allowed to fall, the surfaces of support change from an outward support to a stretch from the underside of the mass. From ancient times the dress was based on the simple principle of suspension from the shoulders or from a waist band. Styles may change but the basic principles remain the same. A piece of material when held up in the air descends by gravity and depends entirely upon its support. When this is taken away it falls, flattens out and becomes inert.

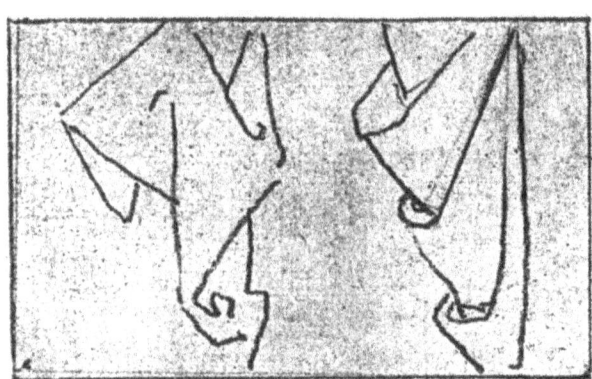